About the Book and Author

The Political Economy of Devaluation: The Case of Peru, 1975-1978
Jorge L. Daly

By the mid 1970s, Peru was in the midst of a serious economic crisis, reflected by a considerable balance-of-payments
deficit, dwindling foreign reserves, and inability to meet
payments on foreign debt. Seeking to reverse the situation and
to keep open external lines of credit, the Peruvian government
negotiated with foreign creditors and later with the International Monetary Fund as part of a larger effort to implement a
new set of economic stabilization policies. One of these policies was devaluation.

This book assesses the impact of devaluation policies on the
economies of developing countries by focusing on Peru's experience during the 1975-1978 period. Dr. Daly first addresses the
theoretical rationale of devaluation, incorporating discussion
of the methodological foundations of the monetary approach to the
balance of payments and its applicability to the Peruvian economy. He then demonstrates how the devaluation of the Peruvian
sol caused a significant reduction in the rate of growth of the
country's GDP and considerably altered the distribution of
national income. The roots of Peru's economic crisis are also
explored from a political economy perspective, and the actual
roles played by monetarist stabilization policies in general and
devaluation in particular are dealt with at length. Finally,
using empirical simulations of alternative stabilization policies, Dr. Daly demonstrates that Peru incurred unnecessary costs
in its attempt to stabilize the economy.

Jorge L. Daly is coordinator of the Latin American Program
in Applied Economics at American University in Washington D.C.

The Political
Economy of Devaluation
The Case of Peru,
1975-1978

Jorge L. Daly

Westview Press / Boulder, Colorado

A Westview Replica Edition

Copyright © 1983 by Westview Press, Inc.

Published in 1983 in the United States of America by
  Westview Press, Inc.
  5500 Central Avenue
  Boulder, Colorado 80301
  Frederick A. Praeger, President and Publisher

Library of Congress Cataloging in Publication Data
Daly, Jorge L. (Jorge Luis), 1950-
   The political economy of devaluation.
   (A Westview replica edition)
   Bibliography: p.
   1. Devaluation of currency--Peru. 2. Peru--Economic policy.
I. Title.
HG895.D34 1983   332.4'14   83-10512
ISBN 0-86531-964-2

Printed and bound in the United States of America.

10 9 8 7 6 5 4 3 2 1

TO XIMENA

Contents

Tables

Acknowledgements

This book has greatly benefited from the intellectual advice of Jim Weaver, Don Bowles, and Richard Weisskoff, who supervised my doctoral dissertation at The American University.

Throughout the research I also enjoyed the advice of Robert Devlin, Jorge Sanguinetty, Efrain González de Olarte, and Stephen Guisinguer. The task of data gathering turned out to be costless thanks to the collaboration of Otto Schulz, José Luis Daly Sr, Julia Daly, Juan Luis Daly, José Luis Daly Jr., Alex Daly, Javier Daly, Jaime Daly, Fiquín Daly, and Tula Daly. The computing skills of Alberto Verme considerably decreased the time spent on the empirical work. I am grateful as well to Cynthia Steele, Jody Williams, Julie Domike, and Salvador Cortés for their help in editing and to Gladys Salazar who assisted in typing the manuscript.

Finally, this intellectual venture was made possible thanks to the emotional support of many friends who constantly encouraged me. The support of Ximena Sepúlveda-Daly, Beatrice Liebenberg, Stephen Richter, and Nery Barrientos was invaluable and unforgettable. To all of them, thank you very much.

Jorge L. Daly

I
Introduction

The objective of this study is to evaluate the economic consequences of the devaluation of the Peruvian sol. Such an assessment is to be understood within the context of economic
stabilization policies applied during the period 1975-1978.

In broad terms, the analysis of the economic performance
under the stabilization period involves the consideration of two
factors: (1) the analytical and theoretical description of the
underlying development strategy of a typical underdeveloped
country like Peru, and (2) the analysis of the "logic of the
need" for a stabilization policy such as the ' one carried out in
Peru which, to date, has generated a great deal of controversy.
Implicit in this twofold analysis is the complementary character
of its elements. As recent historical evidence from several less
developed countries (Jamaica, Zaire, Turkey, Egypt, and Mexico)
has suggested, the introduction and application of stabilization
policies evolves as a response in order to correct economic
disequilibrium which is reflected in the national financial
accounts, both internal and external, and also as an attempt to
reduce the rate of inflation. As I shall elaborate later, in
Peru, it was mainly the inability to meet the payments of principal and interest on the external debt that called for the correction of these financial disequilibria induced by the ever growing
deterioration of the current account. Nevertheless, I argue that
these visible financial deficits in the external and fiscal
accounts are merely a reflection of an underlying economic crisis
set off by the application of specific development strategies.
In the case of Peru, such a strategy has emphasized industrialization via import substitution, introduced in the 1960s, and
conventionally regarded as inflationary.

As is well known, the strategy of industrialization via
import substitution demands interventionist policies by the
government. In its aim to reduce external dependency, the
government actively intervenes in the economic sphere, principal-
ly by manipulating a set of relative prices and by establishing
effective rates of protection on imported consumer goods. I
shall focus the core of my investigation on the manipulation of
the exchange rate.

Peru faced a macroeconomic situation, before and during the
stabilization period, typical of many less-developed countries.

After recovering from a slump in 1967-1968 and then applying austere orthodox fiscal measures until 1971, the country began vigorously pursuing the strategy described above. To better achieve its goal, the Peruvian government enjoyed the unprecedented financial support of the foreign-owned banks which were ready to assist it in financing ambitious public investments and expenditures. By 1975, however, a combination of external factors and misguided internal economic policies, that neglected the export sector, increased considerably the proportion of export earnings used to repay the external debt. Soon, the country faced the alternative of refinancing old loans or defaulting on them. The government ruled out default and decided to refinance its outstanding debt, first directly with the commercial banks in 1976 and through negotiations with the International Monetary Fund in 1977 and 1978. As a result of these negotiations, a set of monetary and fiscal stabilization measures were recommended and applied.

At this stage, I feel it necessary to introduce two important points:

1. My analysis will deal mainly with internal phenomena; that is, I shall attempt to assess the impact of a specific internal economic policy which was applied with the aim of "setting prices right" and thus restoring market equilibrium in the external sector. Whether or not the commercial banks and the International Monetary Fund insisted on the application of harsh fiscal and monetary measures as a condition for loan refinancing is not as important for my purpose as is the economic rationale or logic of its implementation and the specific economic goals of such measures. Moreover, the core of the topic does not deal with the analysis of the external factors which affect economic development positively or negatively. However, external factors will be touched upon to the extent that they affect directly or indirectly the specific stabilization policy to be studied.

2. This study will focus exclusively on short-run phenomena, although the descriptive analysis of the performance of the Peruvian economy will definitely allow for recognition of structural change.

Purpose and Importance of the Study

I believe that this study can shed light on the old controversy within the Latin American school of economic development between monetarists and structuralists. The old structuralist thought stressed supply bottlenecks coupled with price inelastic exports as the cause of inflation. On the other hand, monetarist thought recognized the existence of these constraints, but their presence could be only explained by the implementation of inflationary economic policies. According to this position these policies have generally been an expansionist credit policy and persistent government deficit spending. Therefore, promotion of economic development required curbing inflation, and this could be achieved mainly through fiscal and monetary stability. It is no wonder that the Latin American economists in the 1960s were called structuralists in boom periods and monetarists in periods of slump when unusual stabilization policies went into effect. During periods of boom, relative prices, such as the exchange rate are purposefully manipulated, whereas in the slump period, stabilization policies usually have been directed at choking aggregate demand through such policies as devaluation, monetary contraction, and fiscal restraint.

Despite the fact that the theoretical controversy generated by the Peruvian experience centered on the basic tenets of these two approaches, this study is intended to go beyond a mere analytical comparison of Peruvian reality that the two approaches offer. Instead, my goal is to focus on a broader framework which allows for the recognition of the impact of devaluation on the standard of living of the income groups in Peru. For the purpose of the present study, two basic income groups are to be considered: property owners and non-property owners. This classification expresses a division of Peruvian society in which the ownership and control over the means of production play a significant and determining role in the process of the distribution of income. This will become clearer later as the specific methodology to be used is discussed. In this way, I expect to better assess the appropriateness of devaluation as an economic policy.

The usefulness of contrasting structuralists and monetarists lies in the fact that both provide coherent and long-tested theoretical models which differ fundamentally in their assumptions. To better illustrate this point, one can cite the debate between Cline and Schydlowsky.[1] Cline aligns himself somewhat with the view taken by the IMF and the commercial banks which diagnosed the crisis as the existence of excess demand and which therefore advocated the adoption of corrective measures aimed at "cooling off" the economy. Furthermore, Cline sets out to disprove on empirical grounds two basic structuralist postulates: namely, the insensitivity of imports and exports to the exchange rate, and the insensitivity of imports to income. Citing a combination of internal and exogenous factors which brought on the crisis in the external sector, Cline argues that the type of policies applied here were the best under the circumstances, and that the painful social cost in terms of loss of output and the declining income share of some social groups were to be explained by the delay in taking corrective actions. On the other hand Schydlowsky believes that the stabilization policies applied were a failure in the sense that they resulted in unnecessary deflationary policies which ultimately led to the loss of output. For him, the crisis was misdiagnosed, its roots instead being in a too vigorously pursued import substitution strategy which eventually produced a mismatch between the sectors which generate foreign earnings and the sectors demanding them. In this context, any policy aimed at choking off aggregate demand was seen as misguided since the two most dynamic sectors of the economy (industry and services) had idle capacity. Consequently, the proper strategy to ride out the crisis was to be found on the supply side.

However, as expressed above, I hope to extend the scope of this analysis by introducing the effect of devaluation on the standard of living of the two income groups cited above by analyzing how the functional income shares in the national accounts vary with the application of devaluation. As a result, its effectiveness as a policy tool may be judged according to the benefits and costs it confers upon the two different income groups in Peru.

At this point it is appropriate to state the <u>specific aim of this study</u>. By analyzing the fluctuation and manipulation of a specific relative price--the exchange rate--I have formulated the following hypothesis:

During the period of 1975-1978, the devaluation of the Peruvian sol significantly <u>reduced</u> the growth of national output.

The study will focus, therefore, on the detailed analysis of a specific stabilization policy (devaluation) which has been used widely in LDCs as an instrument to correct deficits in the balance of payments. I expect to clearly demonstrate that devaluation, conceived of as an effective policy instrument to restore market equilibrium in the external sector, will lead to output contraction with its costly social side effects. Additional to the presentation of empirical results, however, there are some unsettling problems which I expect to address thoroughly in this study:

1. What were the causes of the deficits in the balance of payments that eventually led to devaluation? Were these causes related to disorderly market phenomena brought about by import substitution strategy? Or are they more closely attached to structural features of the Peruvian economy?

2. Can the Peruvian economic crisis be properly explained solely by disequilibrium in the external accounts? What alternative approaches can be used to adequately explain the crisis?

The first problem will be extensively dealt with in the next two chapters. The bare facts of aggregate indicators will be called upon to provide reasonable answers. The second problem, on the other hand, assumes that external deficits merely conceal a much deeper and more complex crisis which cannot be adequately explained by pure market analysis. In chapter five, an alternative approach which is encapsulated in the concept of mode of accumulation, is suggested.

Methodology

The basic approach taken for this study is empirical. Considerable emphasis is given to Lance Taylor's model dealing with short-term effects of devaluation which he presents in his book <u>Macro Models for Developing Countries</u> (Mcgraw-Hill 1979). A few comments concerning this model are necessary:

1. Taylor's model incorporates specific institutional features which have been largely ignored by conventional macro theory. The latter has been designed as a response to conditions typical of advanced market societies, but its applicability to the economies of LDCs has been brought into question. Implicit in

Taylor's model is the consideration of some stylized facts which
can adequately characterize the economic structure of LDCs:
  a) The agricultural sector has surplus labor and its
demand for products may be price and income inelastic.
  b) The industrial sector is characterized by oligopolistic, mark-up pricing, and interest costs enter into the cost
of production and final price.
  c) There is a distinction between tradeable and
non-tradeable goods. The former may be highly dependent on
non-competitive intermediate imports; that is, dependent on
imported goods which are not likely to have a locally produced
substitute.
  d) For all practical purposes, money is the only
financial asset.
  e) The distributional effects of income are explicitly
dealt with by evaluating the impact of stabilization policies on
the functional shares of wage and profit incomes.
  2. As noted above, the model deals with short-term phenomena.
  3. Taylor's analysis does not rely on the estimation of
parameters by econometric methods. Rather, his model relies on
the use of accounting identities, based on national accounts.
  For the purpose of this study, the methodological principles
which underlie Taylor's model will be followed closely. Therefore, I will not pursue the investigation based on an econometric
model.
  The model developed in this dissertation consists of 13
equations and rests upon the following assumptions:[2]
  1. There is a two-sector economy in which the export sector
produces for the world market and the home goods sector produces
for domestic need.
  2. The price of exports and imports is fixed in foreign
currency while the price of home goods is determined by a mark-up
on the direct costs of production.
  3. The wage-rate is fixed in domestic currency in the
short-run.
  4. Exports and imports are price-inelastic in the short-run.
  5. Only income-expenditure relationships are considered.
This assumption reflects the analytical convenience of isolating
monetary phenomena with the purpose of focusing exclusively on
income effects.
  An overview of the structure of the Peruvian economy should
lead us to conclude that the characteristics described above fit
its case. In effect, for example, Peruvian export earnings
traditionally have come from the mining and agricultural sectors
whereas its domestic industry behaves basically within an oligopolistic market structure and "has been built by import substitution, via protection."[3]
  I now proceed to detail the entire model:

1. Price of Home Goods

$$P_H = (a_{LH}W + a_{MH}P_M) (1 + Z) (1 + V_H)$$

where:

a_{LH}:   input coefficient of labor into home goods
a_{MH}:   input coefficient of imports into home goods
V_H: rate of government's indirect tax
w: wage rate
P_M: home domestic price of imports
Z: mark-up factor

This equation shows that the price of home goods (P_H) is determined by the total cost of <u>inputs</u> per unit of output which is multiplied by 1 plus an entrepreneurial mark-up Z. Now, to get the total cost per unit of output, all factor costs are multiplied by $1 + V_H$.

2.   <u>Price of Exports</u> (P_X)

$$P_X = e(1 -tx) P_X*$$

where:

e: exchange rate of domestic currency for dollars
tx: rate of ad-valorem tax on export
P_X*:   dollar price of exports on world market

This equation shows what exporters actually net: their traded product has a world price which is fixed in US dollars (P_X*) and which is F.O.B. ("free on board"). They surrender their foreign currency earnings at an exchange rate (e) previous to deduction of an ad-valorem tax (tx).

3.   <u>Price of Imports</u> (P_M)

$$P_M = e(1 + t_M) P_M*$$

This equation shows what importers pay. Their imported goods have a world price (P_M*) which is C.I.F. ("cost, insurance, and freight") and is fixed in foreign currency. To buy the goods they get foreign currency at the exchange rate (e) and pay an import tariff (t_M).

4.   <u>Labor Income</u> (Y_W)

$$Y_W = (a_{LH}X_H + a_{LX}X) w$$

where:

a_{LX}:   input of labor per unit of exports
X_H: level of output of home goods industry
X: level of output of export industry

This equation determines the income of labor which is made up of the sum of the unit labor costs in the home goods and export industries multiplied by their respective values of outputs X_H and X.

5. Profit Income (Y_R)

$$Y_R = Z (a_{LH}w + a_{MH}P_M) X_H + (P_X - a_{LX}w) X + e(REM)$$

Where:
e(REM): emigrant remittances in home currency.

According to this equation, profit income is the sum of the following items:

a) Total profits in the home goods industry, which is equal to the profits per unit, given by $Z (a_{LH}w + a_{MH}P_M)$, multiplied by the level of output of the industry (X_H).

b) Total profits in the export sector, which is equal to the export revenue (P_X), from which one has to subtract first the labor input in this sector ($a_{LX}w$) and then multiply the result by the level of output in the export industry (X).

c) Emigrant remittances in home currency. Although in rigorous theoretical terms this item is not applicable to Peruvian reality since official records do not show considerable money inflow from Peruvians working abroad as the cases of Portugal, Turkey, and Yugoslavia would suggest, it nonetheless could be used to represent the existence of capital flight. It is in this sense that this item will be used throughout the empirical analysis.

6. Non-Property Owners' Consumption Expenditures (D_W)

$$D_W = d_W (Y_W - T_W)$$

where:
d_W: share of labor income devoted to consumption
T_W: direct tax on labor income

This equation shows that wage workers consume an amount equal to their income, after subtraction of income tax, multiplied by their average propensity to consume.

7. Property Owners' Consumption Expenditure (D_R)

$$D_R = d_r (Y_R - T_R)$$

where:
d_r: share of profit income devoted to consumption
T_R: direct tax on profit income

This equation is very similar to equation No.6, but it holds for the incomes of property owners.

8. Total Consumption Purchases (C)

$$C = (D_W + D_R)/P_H$$

According to this equation, total consumption purchases are made up of the consumption expenditures of both income groups divided by the price of home goods derived in equation No.1.

8

9. Home Goods Output Level (X_H)

$$X_H = C + I + G$$

where:
I: investment purchases
G: government purchases

10. Private Savings (S_{priv})

$$S_{priv} = (1 - d_W)(Y_W - T_W) + (1 - d_r)(Y_R - T_R)$$

This equation shows how the savings level of the private sector is determined. The two income groups are considered and each type of saving is arrived at by deducting the direct taxes from labor (profit) and multiplying the result by 1 minus the share of labor (profit) income going to consumption; in other words, by multiplying by the share of income which is saved.

11. Government Savings (S_{GOV})

$$S_{GOV}=V_HP_HX_H/(1+V_H)+et_XP_X*X+et_MP_M*a_{MH}X_H+T_W+T_R-P_HG$$

The first term of the equation shows government revenues derived from indirect taxes. The second and third terms show government revenues generated in the export sector and by import tariff for the intermediate imported goods used in the home goods industry, respectively. The fourth and fifth terms denote the direct taxes on labor and profit incomes, respectively. The value of government purchases is subtracted from the net result.

12. Foreign Savings (S_{FOR})

$$S_{FOR} = eP_M*a_{MH}X_H-eP_X*X - e(REM)$$

Savings by foreigners is made up of all purchases made by local industrialists of foreign-made intermediate products that are used in the home goods industry minus the value of local exports (which are imports made by foreigners), minus emigrant remittances.

13. Savings - Investment Identity

$$P_HI = S_{priv} + S_{GOV} + S_{FOR}$$

where: P_HI: value of investment purchases

Taylor assumes that, in the short run, the mark-up entrepreneurial factor Z, the labor consumption propensity d_W, the profit income consumption propensity d_r, and the input-output coefficients a_{LH}, a_{MH}, and a_{LX} are all constant. The idea is to express total consumption, investment, and government purchases as a function of the level of domestic output X_H. After some algebraic manipulation the whole system is expressed and solved in the following equation:

$$X_H=(1/Q)\left\{(X/P_H)\left[(dw-dr)a_LxW+d_rP_x\right]+(1/P_H)\left[d_re(REM)-(dwTw+drTr)\right]+I+G\right\}$$

$$\text{where: } Q = 1 - dw\, a_{LH}W/P_H - d_r \quad \frac{Z}{(1+Z)(1+V_H)}$$

The model has been devised to show that, as opposed to the conventional macroeconomic theory, there is a negative relationship between the exchange rate and domestic output. A key assumption is the different savings propensities among the two income groups: output is likely to fall if the redistribution of real income derived from devaluation is in favor of the group which has a higher propensity to save.

The way this particular model tests our hypothesis is by simulation analysis. First an initial basic solution is worked out with the national accounts balances used as raw data. This initial solution will give the values of the main parameters of the system, such as the input-output coefficients and the mark-up factor. Thereafter, the values of key variables, such as exports, the exchange rate and the wage rate, are modified according to their real variation in order to show the effect of devaluation on home goods output (X_H). In this way, I will be able to assess the predictive ability of the model by contrasting its results with the actual experience.

Whereas this model places unusual emphasis on income distribution phenomena, its income categories (wage and profit earners) could prove to be too general for social reality. Peruvian society is made up of social groups not easily defined within these two main categories: i.e., peasants, civil service workers, etc. Constraints on data gathering make the task of detailed income disaggregation somewhat difficult and thus render it beyond the scope of the study. Nevertheless, I expect that the empirical results will provide a general approximation of the social effects of the devaluation policies. Also, I expect that it will be a good start for a more thorough analysis of income distribution.

The Data

Since the core of this study is empirical, the reliability of the data is of paramount importance.

In Peru, there are two sets of data for the national accounts. One is published by the Central Bank and the other is prepared by the Instituto Nacional de Estadistica (INE). Careful examination of both sets of data showed that there is a difference between them in the absolute level of measurement of the national accounts. The data of INE shows an absolute level approximately 10 percent higher than the Central Bank data, although both sets show approximately the same growth rates. The difference resides mainly in the product account. The accounts of the external sector are basically the same in both sets.

In a conversation held with the World Bank staff in charge of the Peruvian Division, they stated that the data put out by the INE is of better quality for the following reasons: (a) it is based on a much more rigorous methodology, thus the data is more reliable; and (b) INE provides the official national accounts under exclusive rights granted by Peruvian law.

For these reasons, throughout this study, the data from INE will be used. However, since the external accounts are basically the same I shall also use data from the Central Bank exclusively related to this sector.

NOTES

[1]William R. Cline and S. Weintraub, editors, Economic Stabilization in Developing Countries (Washington, D.C.: The Brookings Institution, 1981), pp.297-334.

[2]Lance Taylor and Paul Krugman, "Contractionary Effects of Devaluation", Journal of International Economics, 8 (1978), 447.

[3]Ibid.

II
The Peruvian Economy in the 1970s: A Descriptive Analysis

The purpose of this chapter is to present a descriptive analysis of the Peruvian economy, highlighting important features prevailing during the period under investigation. To better achieve this goal, three separate yet interrelated topics will be covered: First, a simple but detailed exposition of the structure of the Peruvian economy, in which I will discuss very briefly the overall composition of output and the pattern of employment. Second, given the paramount importance it plays in any stabilization effort, I shall treat separately the essential characteristics of the external sector. Finally, I shall touch upon the roots and characteristics of the crisis of 1975, which, as stated in the introduction, found its most visible manifestation in a deficit of the balance of payments.

Structural Analysis of the Peruvian Economy

I shall not present an in-depth analysis of the Peruvian economy. A vast literature already exists which points to the all but exhaustive research into the nature of the Peruvian economy. Instead, I shall highlight key structural features which are useful for the purposes of this study.

One of the best ways to characterize the Peruvian society (and economy) is by recognizing the heterogeneity of its elements. By this, I rule out the presence of well integrated, organized, and more or less homogeneous markets that are apt to be found in advanced societies. Instead, the observer could be easily struck by the simultaneous convergence of several distinct Perus--the geographical, the ethnical, the social, and the political.

The best theoretical approximation to capture this characterization is dualism. In fact, one can easily distinguish the two well-defined sectors, a modern and a traditional one. The former presents a productive sector generally associated with relatively high levels of total productivity due to the predominance of market relations of production. This sector developed first through export activities, where it enjoyed all the benefits ...and costs brought by the presence of foreign concerns, and gradually moved into industrial activities which catered their production to the satisfaction of the needs of the emerging domestic market. On the other hand, the traditional sector is plagued by extremely low levels of productivity, widespread poverty, and backward, pre-capitalist relations of production.

To better clarify this overall perspective, it is useful to resort to statistics which can concretely depict the relative participation of both sectors over total output and employment. Alberto Couriel has demonstrated that the bulk of the traditional sector is located in the Sierra, specifically in the social groups which are devoted to agriculture.(1) On the other hand, the modern sector is generally associated with manufacturing, fishing, mining, and public services such as banking. Other economic activities such as construction, commerce, and transport are practiced in both sectors.

Table 1 shows how production of total output and total employment by economic activities has been divided between a corporate and a non-corporate sector. This classification is used by Fitzgerald to provide a good approximation of the concepts of modern and traditional sectors commonly used in the theoretical treatment of dualism. Accordingly, the corporate sector is defined by those economic activities that employ five or more workers and it roughly corresponds to the modern sector. Likewise, the non-corporate sector could be used as an approximation to depict the economic activities in the traditional sector.

TABLE 1

PATTERN OF OUTPUT AND EMPLOYMENT, 1975
(per mille of GDP)

	Corporate	Non-Corporate	Total
Output:			
Agriculture	58	69	127
Fishing	6	1	7
Mining	60	–	60
Manufacturing	235	27	262
Construction	25	36	61
Utilities	11	–	11
Banking	35	–	35
Government	77	–	77
Transport	17	38	55
Commerce	100	50	150
Services	47	108	155
Total	671	329	1000

TABLE 1 <u>continued</u>

	Corporate	Non-Corporate	Total
Employment:			
Agriculture	90	340	430
Fishing	10	2	12
Mining	23	-	23
Manufacturing	50	92	142
Construction	22	22	44
Utilities	4	-	4
Banking	7	-	7
Government	76	-	76
Transport	7	28	35
Commerce	46	69	115
Services	22	90	112
Total	357	643	1000

<u>Source:</u> E.V.K. Fitzgerald, The Political Economy of Peru 1956-1978, (London: Cambridge University Press, 1979), p. 312.

This table clearly illustrates the existence of structural asymmetry with regard to the relative participation of both sectors in output and employment. Overall, the corporate or modern sector accounts for 67 percent of total output although it provides just 36 percent of total employment, whereas the traditional sector produces 33 percent of total output but absorbs 64 percent of total employment.

It is possible, however, to gain richer insights into the dual nature of the Peruvian economy by picking out the two leading and most representative activities of both the traditional and modern sectors, that is, agriculture and manufacturing. <u>Agriculture</u> provides just 12.7 percent of total output although it absorbs 43 percent of total employment. Despite the fact that almost half of the total workforce is tied to the land, its relative contribution to total output is far from impressive. This can be explained by the fact that approximately 54 percent of total agricultural output is produced in the traditional sector, which makes up almost 79 percent of the total workforce in agriculture. The difference is accounted for by the corporate or modern sector, which historically developed around the exports of sugar and cotton.

As opposed to the pre-Conquest years, it is not accurate to depict modern Peru as a typical agrarian society. Nonetheless, given the magnitude of the statistics cited above, it is difficult to visualize as realistic any development effort that does not tackle head on the colossal problems plaguing the countryside: extreme poverty, lack of education, malnutrition, unemployment, etc. Failure to do so inevitably leads to an increased migration to the cities on the coast, especially Lima, where the modern productive units have so far proven to be incapable of absorbing the waves of job-seekers. This fact, coupled with the lack of adequate provision of social services, leads to the conclusion that the strong likelihood of social and political unrest is not to be dismissed.

The last 30 years have witnessed a systematic neglect of the countryside. Not only has the migration from rural areas to cities increased dramatically, but also the country must import foodstuffs. The most serious effort to deal with these problems was undertaken by a reformist military regime in the late 1960s and early 1970s. This regime enacted a thorough land reform which affected the ownership of the large estates that produce sugar, cotton, and coffee for export. However, the scope of the reform barely reached the small plots of subsistence peasants, where the poverty of the soil and the lack of an adequate supply of water are serious constraints for the enhancement of productivity.

With respect to industry, I would like to highlight first one salient feature which is of particular importance because the theoretical rationale of the model presented in the last chapter explicitly assumes it: that is, that the industrial productive units (in the case of Peru many of them associated with transnational corporations) basically behave in oligopolistic ways. In effect, as Carlos Amat y León has estimated, approximately 13 percent of the firms control 77 percent of total industrial output.(2) Moreover, it has been calculated that the 200 largest industrial firms represent 62 percent of total industrial output but absorb only 33 percent of total employment.(3) Likewise, the ten largest firms represent 25 percent of total output but absorb only 5 percent of total employment.(4)

There are some other important features characterizing this economic activity that should not be ignored. First, as Pinzás García explicitly points out, Peruvian industry is dependent on foreign inputs.(5) The consequence of this is that the resultant imports are price inelastic, since they are not likely to be produced locally or find close domestic substitutes. Therefore, the demand by local industrialists for the foreign-made inputs will be largely determined by the volume of industrial production, which in turn is dictated by domestic conditions, in other words, by the level of effective demand. As a result, especially in periods of economic expansion, local industrialists are likely to exert pressure on the balance of payments by a steady demand for foreign exchange which ultimately is solved by the expansion of exports. Second, it is believed that Peruvian industry is characterized by the existence of idle capacity; to this respect, Pinzás García cites the work of Abusada Salah, who has empirically demonstrated that only 19.8 percent of the industrial firms (from a sample that takes into account 73.7 percent of gross industrial product) operate in three shifts.(6) Finally, one can cite the fact that the expansion of Peruvian industry has generated very limited absorption of employment, since utilization of capital intensive techniques were favored.(7)

16

Still another way to present this picture is by incorporating these facts within the historical evolution of the diverse development strategies that the country undertook. Thorp and Whitehead state that the wave of industrialization via import substitution which took hold of Argentina, Chile, Mexico, and Brazil in the 1930s and 1940s arrived relatively late to Peru.(8) By contrast, until the late 1950s, Peru was basically an export-oriented economy, with a predominance of enclaves which had very weak linkages to the rest of the economy and which was run essentially by a laissez-faire strategy. The drive to industrialization was vigorous as expressed by the fact that by 1978 industry's share of total output had risen to 25.1 percent from a low 18.2 percent in 1950 (see Table 2). In the 1960s, the rate of growth of the gross domestic product was around 5 percent which, given the rate of population growth, represented an improvement in per capita terms. Yet, the economic success of this strategy was greatly impaired by the fact that import substitution was limited mainly to consumer goods,(9) discouraging therefore the development of backward linkages. On the other hand, the drive to industrialization demanded a colossal effort by the government, not only in the adoption of specific economic policies (now more Keynesian in style) but fundamentally in the construction of the required overhead, so vital for industry. In Peru, this effort was located almost entirely in the urban areas of the coast, diverting the precious resources which could have been directed towards the improvement of basic services in the traditional sector of the peasantry or in expanding the capacity to export.

TABLE 2

GROSS DOMESTIC PRODUCT BY ECONOMIC ACTIVITY (%)

YEAR	AGRICULTURE	FISHING	MINING	INDUSTRY	OTHER *
1950	23.48	0.27	5.64	18.16	52.45
1960	17.22	1.08	7.81	22.95	50.94
1970	14.66	2.18	7.07	24.74	51.35
1975	12.15	0.72	5.72	26.06	55.35
1976	12.08	0.83	5.95	26.57	54.57
1977	12.10	0.71	7.23	25.56	54.40
1978	12.14	0.86	8.07	25.12	53.81

* Includes construction, electricity, housing, government.

Source: INE, Cuentas Nacionales del Perú 1950-1978.

Whatever the type of development strategy adopted, laissez-faire or industrialization via import substitution, it is clear that Peru remains a society in which contrast and gross inequality are very much in evidence. To support this argument, one can look to the work of Alberto Couriel who has attempted to evaluate the extent to which Peruvian society provides for the basic human needs of its people. In his work, basic human needs are defined as the provision of a balanced diet with internationally recognized nutritional ingredients; Couriel has found that 50 percent of the Peruvian families cannot meet that standard and that approximately 70 percent of them live under conditions of extreme poverty.(10)

All this is not surprising in a country in which the lowest 25 percent of the families draw 3 percent of the total income and the highest 10 percent draw 43 percent.(11)

The Importance of the External Sector

Since the nineteenth century, when the country gained its political independence from Spain, the external sector has played a determinant role in the process of economic development. Thorp and Bertram argue that, historically, export revenue proceeds have provided the main basis for an economic development they label as capitalist.(12)

This is another way of stating that the historical evolution of the Peruvian economy could be defined as being one of export-led growth. The success or failure of this pattern of development is closely related to the capacity that an export-type economy should have to contribute significantly to an even distribution of benefits, to encourage the development of strong backward and forward linkages and to accelerate what Meier calls the learning rate of the economy. To assess that capacity requires the consideration of economic factors, such as the nature of the Peruvian exports, as well as social and institutional factors.

As an example, one should remember the economic bonanza in the 1850s and 1860s which was caused almost exclusively by the export of guano. The great economic expansion however was largely wasted in unproductive consumption; on the other hand, despite the fact that native entrepreneurs were actively engaged in this export activity, the marketing of the product depended on the efficiency of English and French intermediaries. Many of the public works undertaken by the state during that period were financed by those intermediaries. Authors like Eduardo Galeano point to this fact as evidence of the influence of foreign concerns which, by dictating trade agreements, imposed unfair economic terms on the host countries that led to the acceleration of the transference of wealth and surplus from these nations to the industrialized world.(13) Galeano's argument points almost exclusively to the influence of external factors in playing a decisive role in the process of underdevelopment and as such it could be readily associated with dependency theory. However, in-depth examination of these historical facts also reveals internal features which have played a similar role in that process; for example, as has just been indicated, the proceeds from guano exports were not channeled for investment.

By the 1870s, the country was exporting nitrate. In 1876 the world price of this product was very low due to the world-wide recession, so the government decided to expropriate and nationalize the mines in an attempt to control the supply. However, competition from English and Chilean concerns established in Bolivia led to the outbreak of a war in 1879 that culminated in the loss of the mines in 1883 and general social and economic devastation. Therefore, the opportunity to foster growth through the export of this product was lost.

Recent history points to the fact that the bulk of exports still consists almost entirely of primary goods. Until 1975, the so-called non-traditional exports accounted for no more than 9 percent of total exports. This heavy reliance on traditional exports results in serious constraints on the smooth development of the sector:

1.   It is well known that the prices of minerals fluctuate according to the economic expansion of the main traders, in this case, the United States and Western European countries.

2.   With respect to agricultural exports, their relative share of total exports has been steadily declining due to the development of substitutes in advanced countries, but also mainly as a result of constraints in the supply side. In fact, the activities in this sector have long been subject to diminishing returns. Any effort to expand the cultivated area requires costly irrigation projects with long gestation periods.

3.   Likewise, the production of minerals faces similar constraints in the supply side. Expansion of available capacity has come as result of costly investment projects undertaken primarily by foreign firms. However, any increase in capacity is not likely to come overnight since foreign investment involves lengthy negotiations in which an adequate return has to be assured.

4.   Finally, fishing products are restricted by nature. Memories have yet to be erased of the massive overfishing and depredation of anchovies in the late 1960s that resulted from unplanned and unregulated private production.

Table 3 shows that Peruvian exports are diversified. Nonetheless, little relief is to be found in this fact because reliance on primary products persists. Such reliance does very little to lessen dependence on external factors (fluctuation of prices) and on foreign capital to expand supply, given the magnitude of investment projects. On the other hand, the same table does show a remarkable increase in the exports of non-traditional products after 1975. The likelihood of attaining smooth development of the export sector via expansion of these products will be explored in chapter five.

The shift in development strategy which occurred in the early 1960s does not nullify Thorp and Bertram's postulate that the rate of expansion of the economy is linked to the performance of the export sector, since the growth of the emergent local industry was conditioned to the availability of imported goods. It is in this sense that structuralist thought views the failure to achieve self-sustaining industrialization to be caused by the existence of critical bottlenecks in the supply side which end up impairing the capacity of the economy to sustain growth. One of these critical bottlenecks is located in the export sector; in other words, in the inability of the country to secure a steady supply of foreign exchange which is required to purchase the needed foreign inputs.

TABLE 3

EXPORTS BY TYPE OF PRODUCTS (millions of dollars)

	1950 $	1950 %	1960 $	1960 %	1970 $	1970 %	1975 $	1975 %	1976 $	1976 %	1977 $	1977 %	1978 $	1978 %
1. Minerals														
Copper	10	5.2	94	21.7	246.7	23.3	155.7	12.1	227.0	16.7	392.3	22.8	409	21.1
Iron			33	7.6	72.1	6.8	51.9	4.0	63.5	4.7	90.5	5.2	74	3.8
Silver	8	4.1	24	5.5	62.3	5.9	146.3	11.3	145.1	10.6	172.5	10.0	207	10.7
Lead	12	6.2	22	5.1	35.3	3.3	41.9	3.3	63.6	4.7	81.8	4.7	89	4.6
Zinc	10	5.2	17	3.9	48.7	4.6	151.5	11.7	191.5	14.1	163.5	9.5	133	6.8
Sub-total	40	20.7	190	43.8	465.1	43.9	547.3	42.4	690.7	50.8	900.6	52.2	912	47.0
2. Fishing														
Fishmeal			50	11.5	303.5	28.6	155.8	12.1	177.5	13.0	179.0	10.4	192	9.9
Other	14		7	1.6	43.2	4.1	52.4	4.0	23.2	1.7	35.3	2.0	46	2.4
Sub-total	14	7.3	57	13.1	346.7	32.7	208.2	16.1	200.7	14.7	214.3	12.4	238	12.3
3. Agriculture														
Cotton	68	35.2	73	16.8	52.1	4.9	53.0	4.1	70.9	5.2	48.0	2.8	38	1.9
Sugar	30	15.5	48	11.1	60.7	5.8	269.1	20.9	91.2	6.7	74.2	4.3	52	2.7
Coffee	1	.6	19	4.4	43.8	4.1	53.2	4.1	101.0	7.4	196.3	11.4	168	8.7
Sub-total	99	51.3	140	32.3	156.6	14.8	375.3	29.1	263.1	19.3	318.5	18.5	258	13.3
4. Oil	25	12.9	18	4.1	6.8	0.6	43.6	3.4	53.3	3.9	52.2	3.0	180	9.3
5. Non-Tradit.	15	7.8	29	6.7	84.8	8.0	116.2	9.0	153.4	11.3	240.0	13.9	353	18.1
TOTAL	193	100	434	100	1060	100	1290.6	100	1361.2	100	1725.6	100	1941	100

Source: Instituto Nacional de Planificación, Informe No.039-76/INP-OIP.
Organización de los Estados Americanos, Informes Económicos de Corto Plazo, Vol. VII, 1981, Perú.

With regard to imports, it is important to note the steady decline in the share of consumer goods imports, as can be seen in Table 4. From a high of 24 percent in 1950, this share has declined to 9.7 percent in 1975. Another estimate gives an even lower share--7 percent in 1972.(14) This trend is consistent with policies applied to foster industrialization via import substitution. The other side of this, of course, is the newly-acquired dependence on foreign intermediate and capital goods, which, being characterized by complex technology, are not easily substituted in the short run, but at the same time are vital for sustaining production.

In the early 1970s, the state assumed an increased influence over imports. In its drive to undertake massive capital projects aimed at expanding overhead capacity (oil pipelines, irrigation projects, etc.), "by 1973 [it was decided that] 42 percent of imports [would be] channeled through state agencies, though of this 75 percent were for resale to the private sector."(15)

Bringing together the two components of the external sector, it is not difficult to visualize a trade balance affected by exogenous factors. On the one hand, if industrial production is to be sustained, the volume of imports is likely to be rigid in the downward direction. Furthermore, import prices are dictated by conditions on the supply side and historically they have tended to rise. On the other hand, export proceeds have been constrained by fluctuations of world prices and by limited supply capacities. Given these considerations, it is no surprise that deficits in the trade balance--if it is true that they have not been the rule--have appeared with a certain regularity and intensity that made it necessary to call for the adoption of corrective measures.

TABLE 4

IMPORTS BY TYPE OF PRODUCTS (millions of dollars)

	1950 $	1950 %	1960 $	1960 %	1970 $	1970 %	1975 $	1975 %	1976 $	1976 %	1977 $	1977 %	1978 $	1978 %
1. Consumer Goods	42	24.0	80	21.4	73.5	14.2	198.9	9.2	176.4	9.3	172.6	10.2	103.6	8.0
2. Raw materials and inter-mediate products	70	40.0	156	41.8	257.3	49.7	1,171.6	54.5	103.9	54.7	1,049.7	61.7	734.3	56.4
3. Capital Goods	62	35.4	135	36.2	186.8	36.1	780.7	36.2	675.2	35.8	468.6	27.6	458.0	35.2
4. Other	1	0.6	2	0.6	0.8		2.8	0.2	4.3	0.2	8.7	0.5	5.6	0.4
Sub-total	175	100	373	100	518.4	100	2154.0	100	1887.8	100	1699.6	100	1301.5	100
Adjustments					181.2		236.1		212.2		464.4			
TOTAL	175		373		699.5		2390.0		2100.0		2164.0		1600.5	

Sources: Instituto Nacional de Planificación, Informe No.039-76/INP-OIP
Organización de los Estados Americanos, Informes Económicos de Corto Plazo, vol. VII, 1981, Perú.

Finally, to complete the analysis of the external sector, let us view the evolution of the service account, as detailed in Table 5. This table shows the increase in the transactions as a result of the process of industrialization undertaken by transnational corporations which constantly repatriate royalties and dividends. The capital account, shown in the same table, reveals the massive increase in foreign loans which eventually had to be repaid in the short term. The consequence of this was a pressure of such magnitude on the balance of payments that it significantly reduced the options of the government in its effort to correct external disequilibrium and meet the payments of the foreign debt.

TABLE 5

BALANCE OF PAYMENTS (millions of dollars)

		1950	1960	1970	1973	1975	1976	1977	1978
1.	Current Account								
	1.1 Trade Balance	49	- 71	- 68	78.8	-1099.3	-740.5	-438.4	340.2
	1.2 Services	-33	- 90	-244	-312.6	-488.5	-509.4	-544.6	-588.0
	Insurance	-12	- 46	- 80	-47.7	-102.5	-60.8	-56.4	-6.7
	Income on investment	-21	- 34	-143	-180.9	-240.3	-366.4	-426.3	-577.7
	Other	-	- 10	- 16	-84.0	-145.7	-82.2	-61.9	-3.6
	1.3 Other	1	18	30	42.1	49.4	57.9	56.8	56.0
	BALANCE (A)	17	-143	-282	-191.7	-1538.4	-1192.0	-926.2	-191.8
2.	Capital Account								
	2.1 Long-term (B)	- 9	108	95	383.0	1135.1	675.5	673.8	421.3
	Direct investment	- 9	51	- 18	49.4	315.7	170.8	54.1	25.0
	Private loans	1	47	36	20.1	26.6	25.0	15.0	13.8
	Public loans	- 1	8	80	319.5	792.7	547.4	610.7	393.7
	Other	-	1	- 3	-6	-	-67.7	-6.1	-11.2
	Basic Balance (A-B)	8	- 36	-187	191.3	-403.3	-516.6	-252.4	229.5
	2.2 Short term	14	8	51	-124.7	-150.0	-307.7	-1114.3	-75.5
3.	Adjustments	-20	- 6	2	-53.4	-23.4	36.7	17.5	-78.1
	BALANCE	2	- 34	-114	13.2	-567.7	-867.5	-349.2	75.9

Source: INE, Cuentas Nacionales del Perú 1950-1980.

Crisis

In the preceding section, I have attempted to link key features of the structure of the Peruvian economy with the important role that the performance of the external sector plays within it. This relationship should be clearer in this section where the roots and characteristics of the crisis are described.

César Humberto Cabrera defines crisis as a particular economic situation in which the country as a whole is forced to adjust its level of economic activity to its "capacity for purchases in the world market."(16) Although this definition by no means exhausts the very complex phenomena that comprise an economic crisis, it is nonetheless useful at this point, insofar as it directly focuses its attention on what has invariably been the most acute and visible manifestation that "something is wrong in the economy." This, as opposed to Chile and Argentina, has not been runaway inflation, but rather, a serious external disequilibrium.

The roots of the crisis, therefore, have to be related to the determinants of the level of economic activity and the capacity to import. The former is a direct function of society's effort to meet the needs of its population, whereas the latter, as defined by Cabrera, "is the relationship that exists between indices of prices of exportables and importables, multiplied by the index of the volume of exports."(17)

Although somewhat arbitrary, this definition is useful because it serves to dramatize the impact that the entry into the world market exerts upon a less developed country. Intuitively, it is not difficult to see that crises result from persistent deficits in the balance of payments which all but exhaust the capacity and credibility to finance them by borrowing abroad.

Before 1975, there were two instances in the post World War II years in which a crisis occurred: in 1958 and in 1967. In the former, Peru was still under a typical laissez-faire economy, which was export oriented; the deficits in the balance of payments were tackled through deflationary measures and recovery quickly settled in by 1959 and 1960. However, Cabrera suggests that recovery was fostered by the export proceeds coming from investments in the mining sector which had started in 1954. In the 1967 crisis, the country had already embarked on industrialization via import sustitution and, to ride out the crisis, the new military government resorted to strict austerity measures, controlling the volume of imports until 1972.

It is impossible to understand and analyze the nature of the 1975 crisis without considering the very particular nature of the military regime which took power in 1968 and the set of economic and social policies enacted to meet its goals. Never before in its history had the country had a government with ambitious goals and plans aimed at reducing or wiping out external dependency and at guiding the society toward self-sustaining industrialization. To meet these objectives, the military regime undertook long overdue structural reforms, the most important of which were:

1. An agrarian reform which avowedly "broke the back" of the landed oligarchy.

2. Nationalization by expropriation (almost all with compensation) of foreign firms with operations in basic sectors (oil, communications, fishing, mining, etc.).

3. Total state control of the export marketing and progressively greater control over imports (as stated in the previous section, by 1973 42 percent of total imports were channeled through state agencies).

4. Creation of state enterprises which would not only carry out operations previously performed by private foreign and local capital but also would operate in areas vital to sustaining the political support of the regime, such as the state-controlled food shops, whose price policies favored urban groups, but not surprisingly, discouraged production of foodstuffs in the countryside.

5. Establishment of labor stability regulations and provisions for the participation of labor not only in profits but also in equity, etc.

The basic rationale of these reforms was to create a more egalitarian society based on a greater control of the economic surplus by the state, which thus would have the material means to fulfill its goals.

Unfortunately, the model ran into serious difficulties by 1975. Until 1971, the government was able to carry out many of the structural reforms cited above and it did so under strict, orthodox fiscal and monetary discipline. However, leaving aside political factors, it is important to single out the set of pure economic factors which played a role in the gestation of the crisis. External factors did exert influence, as evidenced by the world-wide stagflation of 1974 which depressed the prices of some vital exports, such as copper, and inflated the prices of imports.(18) But it is more relevant to look into those internal causes specifically related to economic policies that might be partially responsible for the unfolding of the crisis.

Although macroeconomic figures often omit details which could be important, it is nevertheless illustrative to examine some aggregate indicators in order to have a sense of the general course of the economy. Table 6 provides such figures. Of importance is the fact that the share of exports on gross domestic product declined just as the share of imports was steadily climbing. Also, by 1976 it was evident that despite a significant boost in investment expenditure starting in 1973, the share of consumption on gross domestic product remained the same. The obvious consequence of this was a fall in the share of national savings on gross domestic product and thus a widening savings-investment gap.

Behind the figures shown by Table 6, however, lies a specific economic strategy. Schydlowsky and Wicht, for example, have characterized the overall orientation of the government as one of neglecting the export sector(19); the fixing of the exchange rate for seven years which greatly favored imports and discouraged exports could be cited as an example of that neglect. Another way to see this is that it has generally been accepted that government policies were designed to foster and stimulate the industrialization of imports. The local industrialists, therefore, were supposed to be the social group to reap the benefits of legal dispositions that gave them a high rate of effective protection for their goods, generous tax concessions for invest- ment, a fixed overvalued exchange rate, and access to credit at a fixed, nominal interest rate. However, until 1973, private invest- ment was at best stagnant. According to Thorp, Boloña, and Herzka this was in essence a reflection of the local industrialists' fear resulting from the increased level of state intervention in the economy.(20) Furthermore, whatever increase there was in capital formation until 1973 was in machinery that was essentially labor-saving.(21)

TABLE 6

GROSS DOMESTIC PRODUCT BY EXPENDITURE (millions of 1973 soles)

YEAR	CONSUMPTION	%	GOV.EXP.	%	INVESTMENT	%	EXPORTS	%	IMPORTS	%	GDP	%
1950	81,006	64	9,648	8	25,058	20	20,798	16	10,207	8	126,303	100
1955	106,616	64	13,008	8	35,812	21	30,214	18	18,713	11	166,937	100
1960	120,100	56	20,860	10	44,289	20	52,111	24	21,597	10	215,763	100
1965	179,510	61	32,428	11	55,034	19	67,350	23	40,778	14	293,544	100
1970	240,220	68	40,053	11	44,704	13	76,152	22	48,533	14	352,596	100
1972	266,665	71	45,677	12	35,564	10	77,488	20	48,893	13	376,501	100
1973	280,600	72	48,407	12	65,595	17	52,596	13	54,639	14	392,559	100
1974	193,197	69	52,792	13	92,319	22	54,173	13	70,548	17	421,933	100
1975	303,375	69	60,458	14	87,903	20	55,494	12	66,157	15	441,073	100
1976	313,773	70	63,757	14	76,690	17	55,549	12	59,782	13	449,987	100
1977	317,887	71	72,658	16	57,205	13	61,971	13	59,983	13	449,738	100
1978	304,479	68	64,966	14	49,130	11	70,749	16	41,854	9	447,470	100

Source: INE, Cuentas Nacionales del Perú 1950-1980.

By the same year it was evident that the government had decided to take a major role in the process of capital formation, given the slow growth of private investment. Projects included oil exploration, the construction of a pipeline, irrigation, housing, and defense. In order to finance these projects, the government chose foreign loans. There are specific explanations for this. First, the greater control over the economic surplus that the state had--via expropriation of foreign firms--did not provide the envisaged resources because some of the most important ventures expropriated, such as the oil fields, were in need of more resources to make them more profitable. Second, there was never any platform or program which could have mobilized the vast number of unemployed and underemployed who could have been put to work à la China. Third, the government enjoyed unprecedented access to external borrowing because there was a financial glut in the capital markets.(22) In fact, the petrodollars that invaded the financial institutions after the oil price hike in 1973 could not find local customers for recycling, given that the developed countries were in recession. Thorp and Whitehead even suggest that massive borrowing helped to sustain aggregate demand in the industrialized world.(23)

The new venture on which the Peruvian state had embarked took the form of a massive increase of imports, both in volume and in value. The export revenues which were expected to arise from the newly developed oil fields, and which were supposed to provide the basis for debt repayment, proved, unfortunately, to be overstated and unrealistic. By 1975, the balance of payments was supported solely by the inflows in the capital account, since the current account deficit was 9.7 percent of GDP (see Tables 5 and 7). Meanwhile, economic and political factors narrowed considerably the options of the government regarding imports. On the one hand, it had already embarked on costly capital projects which could not be abandoned. Also, the government was unwilling to cut defense spending, given the likelihood of a war with Chile. On the other hand, state enterprises were involved in the importation of some items (food, fuel) which had become much more expensive. The government did not pass on their full cost to the consumers for fear of jeopardizing the political support of urban groups. Eventually, the deficits of these enterprises were also financed by external borrowing.

What has been left out of this analysis is the diagnosis of the crisis. As stated in the introduction, Cline and Schydlowsky have opposing ideas about it. The fact that from 1971 to 1976 total capacity rose at a rate of 28 percent a year while production rose at 6 percent (24) seems to lend credence to the Schydlowsky thesis. On the other hand, Thorp, Boloña, and Herzka diagnose and attribute the crisis to a combination of adverse external developments coupled with an internal investment expansion strongly linked to a higher import content and an unresolved export supply constraint. However, the purpose of this study is not to deal at length with the diagnosis of the crisis, since, whatever it may be, the stabilization policies that were applied are entirely based on the belief that there was an excess demand. But this is the topic of the next chapter.

TABLE 7

SELECTED INDICATORS

	1970	1973	1974	1975	1976	1977	1978
1. Rate of Growth of Gross Domestic Product (%)	5.4	4.3	7.5	4.5	2.0	-0.1	0.7
2. Investment (% Share of GDP)							
Private	9.0	8.9	8.3	9.8	9.0	9.0	8.2
Public	4.3	6.8	9.9	8.9	8.4	6.8	5.4
3. Current Account balance (% Share of GDP)	3.0	-1.7	-5.9	-9.7	-8.0	-6.9	-1.5
4. Fiscal Account balance (% Share of GDP)	-1.2	-4.3	-7.5	-7.2	-8.8	-12.4	-7.5
5. Consumer Price Index (variation)	5.0	9.5	16.9	23.6	33.5	38.1	58.0

Source: INE, Cuentas Nacionales del Perú 1950-1980.

NOTES

(1)Organización International del Trabajo (OIT), Perú: Estrategia de Desarrollo y Grado de Satisfacción de las Necesidades Básicas (1978), Chapter Three.

(2)Carlos Amat y León, La Economía de la Crisis Peruana (Lima, Perú: Fundación Friedrich Ebert, Serie Materiales de Trabajo No.16, 1978), p.60.

(3)Claes Brundenius, "Concentración de la Producción y Estructura de la Propiedad". Informe No.040-76 (Lima, Perú: Instituto Nacional de Planificación/INP-OIP, julio 1976), p.57

(4)Ibid.

(5)Teobaldo Pinzás García, La Economía Peruana 1950-1978. Un Ensayo Bibliográfico (Lima, Perú: Instituto de Estudios Peruanos, 1981), p.59.

(6)Ibid., 67.

(7)Ibid., 66.

(8)Rosemary Thorp and L. Whitehead, Inflation and Stabilization in Latin America (New York: Holmes and Meier Publishers, 1979), p.111.

(9)Pinzás García, op.cit., p.42.

(10)Organización Internacional del Trabajo, op.cit., p.5.

(11)Amat y León, op.cit., p.73.

(12)R. Thorp and G. Bertram, Peru 1890-1977: Growth and Policy in an Open Economy (New York: Columbia University Press, 1978), p.321.

(13)Eduardo Galeano, Open Veins of Latin America; Five Centuries of the Pillage of a Continent (New York: Monthly Review Press, 1973).

(14)R. Thorp, C. Boloña, and C. Herzka, "The Balance of Payments Adjustment Problem in Peru 1974-1978", (unpublished manuscript, 1978), p.5

(15)Ibid., 14.

(16)C. H. Cabrera, Perú: La Crisis y la Política de Estabilización (Lima, Perú: Fundación Friedrich Ebert, Serie Materiales de Trabajo, No.17, 1978), p. 13.

(17)Ibid., 16.

28

(18)Thorp, Boloña, and Herzka, op.cit., pp.3-9.

(19)Daniel Schydlowsky and Juan Wicht, Anatomía de un Fracaso Económico (Lima, Perú: Universidad del Pacífico, Centro de Investigación, 1979), Chapter Two.

(20)Thorp, Boloña, and Herzka, op.cit., p.20

(21)John Sheahan, "Peru: International Economic Policies and Structural Change, 1968-1978", (unpublished manuscript), p. 12.

(22)An excellent study on the role of external borrowing is provided by Robert Devlin, Los Bancos Transnacionales y el Financiamiento Externo de América Latina: La Experiencia del Perú 1965-1976 (Santiago, Chile: Comisión Económica para América Latina, CEPAL, 1980).

(23)Thorp and Whitehead, op.cit., p.5.

(24)Sheahan, op.cit., p.12.

III
Survey and Theoretical Rationale of Stabilization Policies

As stated in the introduction, stabilization policies are undertaken in an effort to correct the disequilibrium in the external sector and to control inflation. It is important to highlight the fact that by 1975 foreign creditors were no longer willing to pump loans into the Peruvian economy. There are various reasons which might explain this sudden turnabout in foreign lending. Of particular relevance were the new tightness in financial markets which appeared in 1974-1975, the growing suspicion that the promised oil potential was greatly overestimated, and finally, the huge deficit in the current account (see Table 7). Whereas in 1973 suppliers of capital had suddenly flooded the country with loans in their eagerness to find customers able to absorb the liquidity surplus, by 1975 the behavior of foreign banks all but precluded the granting of loans needed to finance the current account deficit.

The government chose to correct this imbalance via policies aimed at cutting aggregate demand. In this chapter I will first spell out, in broad terms, the policies applied between 1975 and 1978. Second, I shall deal extensively with the theoretical rationale that underlies the logic of the implementation of the stabilization policies that were applied in Peru during that period. For the purpose of this study, I will put special emphasis on the theory of devaluation. Finally, I shall briefly explore an issue whose paramount importance should become evident later: on strict theoretical ground, what is the usefulness and applicability for a country like Peru of the typical stabilization policies that are based on a specific vision of the world? My objective is to break ground and unveil an approach to assess Peruvian reality which essentially is structuralist at heart and which will be covered extensively in the following chapter. Nevertheless, this issue will not be put to rest in this chapter. I hope to have proven that the nature of the Peruvian crisis and the subsequent remedies applied should be understood within a broader framework that incorporated social and institutional as well as purely economic factors. This framework will provide a better understanding of the roots of the Peruvian crisis as well as the consequences in terms of the efficiency and social cost that the stabilization policies entailed.

Survey of the Stabilization Policies[1]

For all practical purposes the stabilization period started in Peru in 1976. The government decided to enter into direct negotiation with its main lenders--basically US and European Banks. The objective was to secure a loan to support the balance of payments and restructure the payment of the foreign debt. As a gesture of seriousness, the government decided to cut the fiscal deficit, and, to this end, some prices were raised by eliminating various subsidies and by introducing new indirect taxes.

In June 1976, a devaluation of the sol was decreed as a measure to correct the deficit in the current account. The new parity went from S/.45 to S/.65 per US dollar and in September of the same year the system of mini-devaluations was introduced to keep stimulating export activities. The objective was to prevent a deterioration in the competitive position of Peruvian exports stemming from a rising price level. Simultaneously, the government decided on a sharper attack on the fiscal deficit: a 105 percent increase in the price of gasoline was enacted in order to correct the finances of PETROPERU (the state firm in charge of marketing) and similar increases were introduced for the prices of food items which were marketed by a state agency. Also, it was decided to freeze all public investment projects whose gestation periods went beyond 1978, and to reduce current expenditures. Finally, restraint in granting credits to the private and public sectors was also implemented.

The other side of the agreement with the foreign banks was that the government was able to secure a loan of $400 million. However, negotiations with the private banks broke off early in 1977 with the complaint that the government was not enforcing the fiscal cuts. The overall fiscal deficit by the end of 1976 was 8.8 percent of the gross domestic product (see Table 7). As should be clearer later, the protests of the banks were not unfounded since it was obvious that the government was either unwilling or incapable of making substantial inroads to correct the fiscal deficit. The legitimacy of the banks' complaints, however, becomes moot when the political and economic realism of such a new policy option is considered. This point is addressed explicitly by Thorp, Bolona, and Herzka. In any case the consequence of all this was that the banks demanded that the government request IMF help to develop a mutually agreed-upon set of policies to rapidly correct the financial disequilibrium. This would help to restore the confidence of the banks in the ability of the country to meet the payment of past and future loans.

The negotiations with the Fund proved to be painful, lengthy, and of course, not devoid of heated political discussions. The situation facing the government was desperate, to say the least, since its reserves, which it had drawn upon heavily, were now negative. As is generally accepted, this indicator plays a very important role in the attitude of foreign banks towards their debtors. Considering that the government had ruled out default, it had no choice but to try to strike an agreement with the Fund that would be the least socially painful, but which would permit it to refinance payments and to secure future loans. Unfortunately, the measures that were eventually applied were very painful socially, at least for a substantial part of the population, as will be revealed later. What is most unfortunate however, is the fact that there is no evidence whatsoever of a fundamental dis-agreement between the Fund and the government regarding the types of stabilization policies to be applied. Evidently, the disagree-ment between the two institutions was not to be found in either the rationale or in the applicability of the corrective measures. Instead, I argue that whatever disagreement existed was one of degree and intensity. For the government, this was of critical importance since, on one hand, it was entirely committed to pursu-ing its objectives (from which the purchase of weapons is not to be omitted)--almost entirely concentrated on solving the crisis in the external sector--but, on the other hand, it had to deal with a situation of increased social unrest. If this conjucture is not clear by now, let us review the events of 1977.

An agreement with the IMF was not reached until June 1977. Before that, disagreements centered around the extent of cuts in government expenditures, the devaluation rate, and the amount of credit to be granted to the public sector. Finally, when an agree-ment was reached that included the types of measures described above plus a further increase in the prices of food and gasoline, it set off a massive social protest which culminated in a general strike that paralyzed the country. It was then that the government backed off and decided to abandon the mini-devaluation scheme and reintroduce some subsidies.

The situation did not improve and a new accord was struck with the Fund in which it was agreed that, although some of the subsidies were to be kept, the government should undertake sub-stantial cuts in public expenditures to try to reduce signifi-cantly the fiscal deficit. In the external sector, the government decided to float the sol. However, early in 1978 it was evident that the fiscal deficit was still 12.4 percent of the gross do-mestic product and the external deficit on the current account was 6.9 percent of the gross domestic product (see Table 7). On the basis that the government did not enforce the required cuts in public expenditures, negotiations stalled and fell through by February 1978.

The scope of the study covers this period. Throughout this discussion it is possible to distinguish clearly an underlying concept ruling the rationale of the policies applied. That con-cept is demand contraction, and its associated policies are fiscal restraint, monetary restraint, and devaluation. To con-sider this, let us turn to the next section.

Theoretical Rationale

In the previous section it was stated that the stabilization policies typically applied are based on a specific vision of the world; in other words, on a particular doctrine. I argue that such a doctrine is monetarism.

Stabilization policies, as will be discussed extensively in later chapters, could be understood not only as measures aimed at correcting financial disequilibrium and at reducing the rate of inflation but also as a concentrated economic effort to restore profitability in critical productive sectors that may well require a shift in the general development strategy. Authors like Jürgen Schuldt argue that in Latin American countries, especially in those of the Southern Cone, there has been a profound transformation in the general orientation of their economic policies in the last 30 years that basically corresponds to the rearranging of their pattern of economic growth. The purposeful goal of this transformation has been to lay the ground work for a more dynamic accommodation of the leading productive sectors to the demand requirements of the international markets, which invariably constitute the prime source for growth. According to this evolution, as I shall elaborate below, stabilization policies applied in the 1970s come much closer to the basic tenets of monetarism than those applied in the 1950s. This is true with respect to Chile, Argentina, and Uruguay; the same fact holds for Peru although with somewhat different characteristics, given the fact that, in the late 1950s, this country was still under an export-led economy. Let me elaborate.

As stated in the first chapter, there were two opposed schools in Latin America which provided explanations for the causes of inflation: the structuralists and the monetarists. This debate florished as the leading Latin American countries heartily embarked on the process of industrialization via import substitution that was to result in abnormally high levels of inflation in the 1950s. What is of special interest is to show the evolution of the stabilization policies between the 1950s and 1970s and to see how closely they are attached to monetarism. I believe that the nature of the Peruvian case, being structurally different from the countries of the Southern Cone, may be understood better in light of the historical debate that took place in the 1950s and which was renewed in the 1970s.

There is extensive literature which deals with monetarist thought, though this is not the place to review it. However, some basic tenets are worth bearing in mind; among them: the rescue of the old quantity theory of money to show that, with velocity essentially constant, nominal income is determined by a multiple of the money supply; that private spending in consumption and investment is essentially stable as derived from a demand for money which also is stable and which exerts a direct control over national income (money is all-powerful); that, as believed in the classical world, relative prices, wages, and the rate of interest are _flexible_, downward as well as upward; that the economy is basically stable, especially if left to the rational decisions of maximizing productive agents and consumers; and, consequently, that government intervention hampers the overall welfare of society by obstructing the efficient mechanism of free market forces.

In the 1950s, however, I have found no evidence that advocates of stabilization policies were strongly attached to all the principles just described. For example, Brazilian economist Roberto Campos rejects the belief that monetarism in Latin America follows the tenets of classical liberalism and that it ignores the existence of structural unemployment.(2) Rather, all or most of the emphasis of this doctrine is centered around the idea that the pervasive structural bottlenecks (food and foreign earnings) are likely to persist if there is no purposeful economic action that creates an atmosphere of stability. In fact, price stability is seen as a precondition for sustained growth and development. Associated with this is the recognition that structural reform --such as in land tenure and improvement in human and social overhead capital--is badly needed, and that an appropriate fiscal-monetary policy mix must be implemented, aimed primarily at curbing an inflation seen as being essentially demand-pull, and at taxing the consumption of luxuries.

It is not unreasonable to argue, therefore, that monetarist thought in the 1950s should be viewed not so much as an elaborate body of concepts rigidly owing its precepts to classical liberalism, but rather as a specific strategy pragmatically associated with immediate economic action. This becomes more evident when bearing in mind that the application of stabilization policies came when the failure of the strategy of industrialization via import substitution had become apparent to all: erratic fluctuation of the prices of important items (food, energy, transport, wages, rents, etc.); acceleration of inflation; deceleration of the overall growth rate of the economy; speculation and acceleration of capital flight; investment in quick-yield ventures, most of an unproductive nature (luxuries, real estate, etc.); accumulation of inventories; balance of payments and fiscal deficits. Therefore, the direct roots of monetarist action can be traced to the economic distortions produced by a vigorously applied strategy that had run into a dead end. But, the flaws of the strategy in this period of stagflation--and thus the rise of monetarism--are not as important as the failure of the policy-makers associated with structural analysis to provide adequate and realistic programs of alternatives to get the economy out of the crisis without incurring high social and economic costs. In other words, since structural thought is more inclined to stress the bottlenecks and constraints existing in the supply side, its analyses and diagnoses--though in my judgement richer and more accurate than those of its monetarist counterpart--fell short of advocating policy actions specifically designed to remove the supply constraints. It is not easy to explain this historical failure. What is evident, however, is that any attempt to address this vital issue invariably has to touch upon often thorny political considerations which end up, at the very least, in questioning the structure of power in the society, and therefore trascending the frontiers of pure economic analysis. To illustrate, structural thought would attribute the cause of runaway inflation to stagnation in the agricultural sector which, given its importance in providing food-stuffs for urban workers, limits (in a closed economy) the rate of growth of industry. Attempts to improve food supply could run into structural difficulties of an institutional nature, such as the land tenure regime and the government's resource allocation between urban and rural areas. Another example might be the recognition of a foreign exchange bottleneck. Improvements in export capacity are hampered if the country trades within an international order often depicted as enforcing adverse terms of trade

for typical export products. As might be expected, the advocacy
of international reform in this area or the reorientation of efforts toward more inward-looking development strategies clashes
with foreign and local vested interests.

There were some particular circumstances, however, in which
there was direct and effective government action to remove the
supply constraints. This was achieved through property reform;
the rationale was that if the state could own and control those
resources which in private hands were the source of bottlenecks,
it could allocate them in such a way as to enhance total productivity for the direct benefit of the underprivileged. The govern-
ments of Frei and Allende in Chile and the military regime in
Peru are two classic examples of this effort. Nevertheless, a
characteristic of these regimes was also the implementation of
income distribution policies (in favor of the workers), which at
one point had to be accomodated with the goal of sustaining economic growth. This task, unfortunately, proved to be more difficult than expected, given the failure of private investors to
expand production; among the many reasons that can explain this
fact, one can cite the fear of institutional change and the runaway inflation that the process generated. Therefore, sustaining
economic growth and maintaining the redistributive policies were
primarily supported by government deficit spending; given the
fact that, for all practical purposes, the absence of well-devel-
oped financial markets rules out the effectiveness of a sale of
government bonds in open market operations, this government spending in all likelihood was financed by borrowing directly from the
Central Bank. This leads to an expansion of the money supply,
which in the presence of government projects of long-gestation periods, waste and a weak production response in the supply of critical goods (such as foodstuffs), invariably leads to inflation.

Given the failure of structuralist policies to solve the economic crisis in the short-run, the monetarist approach quickly
provided the rulers with a viable set of policies directed at controlling runaway inflation and thus create an atmosphere of price
stability that would restore confidence to the private sector in
general and profitability to the export and agricultural sectors
in particular. In the 1950s and 1960s these policies were concentrated in the elimination of the manipulation of the set of
relative prices that were not reflecting their true opportunity
costs, and in solving a general economic situation of excess
demand, that is, a situation where aggregate demand had outpaced
aggregate supply and which was seen as the source of the generation of inflation. In order to eliminate price controls, in other
words, "set prices right," monetarist policies prescribed the reliance on free market forces; this goal contemplated the elimination of subsidies on items such as foodstuffs, transport fares,
rents, etc. and, more importantly, the devaluation of the exchange
rate since it was widely believed to be overvalued, and as will be
shown below, would foster the recovery and enhance the profitability of the export sector. This last policy is also applicable and
used as an instrument for the elimination of excess demand. In
principle, it was argued, such imbalance would be solved if trade
liberalization were introduced, which would lead to the purchase

of foreign goods, substantially less expensive than the locally produced substitutes. However, this view did not consider the fact that financing and payment for these imports could pose a real financial problem if, as structuralist thought strongly believes, the country had real bottlenecks in the export sector, in other words, an inability to generate a steady inflow of foreign exchange.

In the 1950s and 1960s, monetarist policies relied on three traditional instruments to reduce aggregate demand. They are monetary restraint, fiscal restraint, and devaluation. I shall define and explain briefly these instruments below.

Monetary Restraint

It is seen as the main mechanism to halt inflation, in essence "a monetary phenomenon." The main way to achieve this is by tightening credit and thus reducing real liquidity. This in turn would aid in the process of creating an atmosphere of price stability and would foster growth.

One of the typical instruments for tightening credit is the manipulation of the rate of interest; by raising it, it is presumed that consumption and low-yield investment will be discouraged, and that savings will increase. An inflow of capital is also expected. On the other hand, as Taylor clearly points out,(3) this policy is directly responsible for an increase in the price level since interest costs enter into prime production costs and, given the oligopolistic nature of industry, are likely to be passed on to the consumer. The overall consequence is that higher interest rates, coupled with measures to restrict demand, are likely to lead to stagflation.

Fiscal Restraint

The objective of this policy is the elimination of the persistent budgetary deficits, which being essentially financed by borrowing directly from the Central Bank, are seen as one of the primary sources of inflation. Not only is the fiscal deficit seen as exerting strong pressure on the monetary accounts but also, specifically in the Peruvian case, as exerting pressure on the balance of payments through imports.

The best way to curb this type of demand is by balancing the budget. This can be accomplished by:

1. Cutting current expenditures.
2. Raising taxes.
3. Financing the state enterprises providing goods and services (i.e., food, transport) through non-inflationary ways; that is, by raising the prices of those products.

In situations of great disequilibrium, even cutting government investment is advocated. With regard to taxation, the norm usually followed has been the increased taxation on sales, since it is the most secure way of getting additional revenue. Increase in revenues via direct taxes are of a more complex nature, but pains are taken to insure that they do not affect those productive sectors that are supposed to speed up recovery by enjoying attractive rates of profitability.

Devaluation

This policy is of unusual importance for this study since the empirical model which is presented in the next chapter has been structured around the purposive manipulation of the exchange rate. For this special reason, I shall explore the theoretical postulates of exchange-rate adjustments in some detail. In what follows, it is assumed that our economy is relatively small vis-à-- vis the rest of the world and that its exchange rate is fixed by the monetary authorities. These premises hold true for the actual experience of the Peruvian economy.

In general terms, devaluation of the domestic currency is a policy that aims directly at correcting a deficit in the balance of payments. Following the standard precepts of macroeconomic theory,(4) devaluation is an ideal and effective policy under conditions of less than full employment of resources, of persistent balance of payment deficits, and under conditions where flexibility of wages and relative prices are not present. If the given goals of the society are to attain full employment and equilibrium in the balance of payments, then devaluation helps the society to move closer to those goals.

I shall illustrate this effect by using the tools of conventional Hicks-Hansen analysis. According to this theoretical framework, simultaneous equilibrium in the product market--where intended investment is equal to savings--and in the money market-- where the demand for money balances is equal to the money supply-- is attained at a given rate of interest and at a given level of income. This is represented in the well known diagram that relates the rate of interest and the level of income; the product market is represented by the IS curve which shows the combinations of the rate of interest and level of income when the product market is in equilibrium, and, as is well known, has a negative slope. Similarly, the money market is represented by the LM curve which has a positive slope showing all the combinations between the rate of interest and the level of income in which there is equilibrium in the money market. The intersection of both curves will determine the rate of interest and also the level of income, which, however, could be well determined at less than the level of full employment.

The external sector can be easily incorporated within this framework. This is done by establishing the balance of payments function which is dependent on the following variables:

1. The level of exports, which is explained by the price level and the exchange rate.

2. The level of imports, which is dependent on the price level, the exchange rate, and the level of income; and

3. Capital inflows, which are positively related to the rate of interest.

The balance of payments function is represented by a curve which has a positive slope and which represents all the combinations between the rate of interest and the level of income for which the balance of payments is in equilibrium, in other words, equal to zero. All the points below the curve represent a situation of external deficit whereas all the points above it represent a surplus.

Now let us imagine a situation in which the economy attains simultaneous equilibrium in the product and money markets and in the external sector, but at an income well below the full employment level. Assuming that wages and prices are rigid in the downward direction, devaluation is a useful tool to move the economy towards the direction of full employment equilibrium. Accordingly, devaluation will induce a shift in relative prices that should make the country's exports more competitive abroad because they would now be cheaper in terms of foreign currency; this increase in exports will shift the IS curve to the right. At the same time, the increase in net exports leads to an expansion in the money supply (a shift in the LM curve to the right) and the balance of payments curve should move to the right as well reflecting an equilibrium in the external sector at a higher level of income, originally induced by the increase in exports. In this way, the economy will move to the level of full employment with external equilibrium. The appropriateness of devaluation as a policy becomes more relevant when the latter condition is not present, for example, when there is a deficit in the balance of payments; in this case, the move towards full employment is necessarily accompanied by the reduction of the external deficit since devaluation would lead to the increase in the total value of exports in foreign currency and to a reduction in the total value of imports, also in foreign currency.

There are distinct and opposing views of devaluation as a mechanism to achieve balance of payments equilibrium. To my mind, the most important are the elasticity approach, which is inspired by Marshallian analysis; the absorption approach, which closely follows Keynesian analysis; and finally, the monetary approach which follows in the footsteps of the monetary approach to the balance of payments. First I shall briefly discuss the elasticity and absorption approaches to devaluation, which validate the need for some sort of government intervention to correct the inability of the pure market mechanism to automatically adjust the balance of payments. The monetary approach will be discussed later, in the context of the monetarist policies of the 1970s that rely so heavily on the theoretical foundations of the monetary approach to the balance of payments.

Briefly, the elasticity approach treats devaluation by analyzing the relative price changes induced by exchange-rate adjustment on the value of exports and import flows. In this approach, the aim is to correct the current account deficit and this will depend on the elasticities of the tradeable products.

Devaluation essentially means that a unit of foreign currency, e.g. the US dollar, has become more expensive in terms of the local currency, in this case, the Peruvian sol. On the side of imports neither the supply in dollars nor the demand in soles is affected by devaluation; what is affected is the demand in dollars and the supply in terms of soles. Dollar prices being unchanged, the decline in dollar outpayments will be determined by the extent of the decline in the volume of imports which, as is known, is the price-elasticity of imports. Only when the latter is totally inelastic, i.e., when the demand curve for imports is vertical, will total outpayments be the same since prices in soles will rise by the same proportion of devaluation.

On the side of <u>exports</u>, they will now be relatively cheaper in terms of dollars so that a competitive edge could be gained. The extent to which devaluation produces an increase in dollar in payments depends on the price-elasticity of foreign demand for Peruvian exports. If this demand is elastic, the lower dollar price of Peruvian exports will be greatly outweighed by an increase of sales that will lead to an increase in export revenues. However, if the foreign demand is price inelastic, exactly the opposite occurs, since a lower dollar price of exports brings less revenue than before.

The famous Marshall-Lerner condition, therefore, states the conditions for which devaluation brings about an improvement in the balance of payments. Given an infinite elastic supply of exports and also an infinite elastic supply of imports, there will be an improvement in the trade balance if the elasticity of demand for the country's exports plus the elasticity of demand for the imports exceeds unity.

Associated with this improvement in the balance of payments, devaluation theory predicts an increase in income as well. On the side of exports, devaluation should produce a decline in the local consumption of these products because, under the assumption that they are produced with conditions of increasing costs or with a higher import content, they will now be relatively more expensive in terms of soles; the consequence of this is the immediate release of units which can now be sold abroad, thus seizing the higher competitiveness abroad. Equally important is the fact that the greater competitiveness of exportables should induce a resource reallocation in the producing sectors in the direction of production of exportables. On the other hand, the relatively greater expense of imports in terms of dollars means that the locally produced substitutes are now relatively cheaper. Again, there is an incentive for transferring resources to the production of the latter to increase income and employment at home.

Therefore, it can be seen that the elasticity approach views the success of devaluation as operating exclusively through the effects on relative prices. The success is more strongly felt when the economy is facing an external deficit under a situation of less than full employment. Given the correct elasticities, devaluation induces a higher output in exportables and in import substitutes, which should reflect a higher total income, output, and employment. However, accompanying these effects is a rise in the price level which partially offsets the greater competitive advantage brought about by the devaluation. If the economy is already at full employment, the devaluation will not affect output but rather will produce an increase in the price level of the same magnitude of devaluation. Even if the economy is at less than full employment, an increase in the price level is expected from the rise of the price of exportables and from the price of those products which use imported products as inputs. In any case, the full success will be impaired by the extent of inflationary pressures. If the increase in the inflation rate matches the devaluation rate, then the competitive gain will vanish--whether this inflation increase is due to higher prices of imported inputs, to wage increases, to the budget deficit, or to expectations.

The <u>absorption</u> approach, on the other hand, is based on the use of national real income identity to assess the likely effect of devaluation. Let

$Y = C + I + G + (X-M)$ where:

Y = real income; C = consumption; I = investment; G = government expenditure; $X-M$ = trade balance.

Furthermore, let

$C + I + G = A$,

denoting the domestic expenditures on locally produced goods. So,

$Y = A + (X-M)$

If the economy is at less than full employment, any improvement in the trade balance as a result of devaluation will be reflected in higher real income (Y) as long as this improvement is larger than the increase in domestic absorption (A). This is only possible when the overall marginal propensity of the population to consume is less than one. However, if the economy is at full employment, an improvement in the trade balance must necessarily be accomodated by an equal decrease in (A). Unless the authorities apply fiscal and monetary measures that cut aggregate internal spending, the effect of devaluation will be reflected in the rise of the price level which will wipe out the competitive advantages induced by devaluation, thus preventing the release of resources in the non-tradeable sector from being transferred to the tradeable sector.

Under this approach, therefore, a devaluation will be successful in improving the balance of payments (in foreign currency terms) "...only to the extent that the inflation of domestic currency prices incidentally reduces the excess of absorption (real expenditure) over (real) income".(5) This, of course, is the situation commonly depicted as a "country living beyond its means," because if $X-M < 0$, this necessarily means that $Y < A$. And the success in reducing real expenditure will be the better when the marginal propensity to save is high and when the government extracts higher revenues through taxes.

At this particular stage, it is my purpose to integrate the key features of the stabilization policies applied in the 1970s. It should be remembered that it was postulated above that in this period, stabilization policies present a closer adherence to monetarism than the ones that were undertaken in the 1950s. This difference resides mainly in the fact that the 1970s have witnessed a much more radical application of the precepts of the classical doctrine as it is evidenced by the drastic reduction of the public sector (Chile is a clear example) and by the higher degree of openness of the economies to the international markets. The brief discussion that follows attempts to explain these phenomena.(6)

In the 1970s, monetarist policies should be properly understood as a radical attempt to solve a profound economic crisis that had greatly threatened the stability of the existing social and political institutions. This attempt is a response to the disequilibria in the external and internal accounts which were of a much more serious magnitude that the ones in the 1950s. This point is not difficult to prove as is evidenced by the great difference between the Chilean inflation rates of the 1950s and the ones in the later 1960s and early 1970s. To tackle this disequilibrium, the drastic reduction of the public sector and the reallocation of resources to the private sector is strongly advocated, as well as the "liberalization" of the rate of interest which thus would lead to the creation of much more dynamic local financial markets.

There are, therefore, two major differences that separate the stabilization policies of the 1970s from those of the 1950s. The first of these has to do with the political environment. In countries like Chile and Argentina, the magnitude of the economic crisis was undermining the stability of the social institutions and the implementation of a socialist state was feared; given this fact, the stabilization policies that were eventually implemented were invariably accompanied by authoritarian political regimes which ended up smashing the gains and aspirations of the social groups most favored by the structuralist or import substitution policies (workers, local industrialists). The consequence of this is that, as opposed to earlier experiences, in the 1970s monetarist measures are no longer short-term economic policies but, on the contrary, they constitute the rational foundation for a long-term plan devised to reorient the pattern of economic growth in a way that drastically reduces government intervention in the economic arena. The validity of this point should become more apparent when I return to it in later chapters.

The second major difference lies in the purposeful and rigorous application of trade liberalization policies. This goal, in fact, is entirely consistent with the reorientation of the pattern of economic growth since there is a shift away from protectionism and import substitution policies in favor of a development strategy that places more importance on the development of exports. It is in this sense that the greater importance of monetarism in the 1970s can be directly related to specific social and economic phenomena that have resulted in the application of this doctrine as an effort to legitimize and instrumentalize particular economic policies that are different from the ones stressed in the development strategies of the 1950s. I will return to this point in later chapters.

Trade and financial liberalization have found their theoretical expression in the refinements and developments that took place in monetarist thought in the late 1960s and early 1970s. Such refinements are primarily concentrated in the theoretical formulations of the monetary approach to the balance of payments. A discussion of this theory follows.(7)

This approach, as opposed to other views, places unusual emphasis on the role of money. According to this approach the familiar components of the balance of payments--current account and capital account --are completely ignored and lumped together into one "above the line" category. This "above the line" category represents in essence an item that should settle any difference between total outpayments and inpayments derived from the autonomous transactions that take place in the external sector. Usually this item is represented by foreign reserves and shows the "effect of a balance of payments deficit or surplus in the domestic monetary base.(8)" The latter, in turn, is made up of banks' reserves and currency in the hands of the public and determines the money supply.

The approach rests upon the following assumptions:(9)

1. The demand for and the supply of money are stable functions of a few variables. Of particular importance is the fact that money is a stock and the demand for it is a positive function of nominal income.

2. To achieve macro-equilibrium in the long-run, stock and flow-equilibrium should exist in all markets.

3. Output and employment are determined by the real forces (just as in the classical world) and they tend toward full employment equilibrium.

4. Perfect substitution and free movement of goods and services in product and capital markets insure that there is one single universal price for a specific product (law of one price). This key premise is derived from the assumption that the economy is small vis-à-vis the rest of world and, therefore, it is a "price taker." In other words, it can control neither the prices of products nor the interest rate. Therefore, the domestic interest rate should be the same as the foreign interest rate and the local price level should equal, as well, the world price level.

Central to this approach is the active role that money plays, in the sense that what essentially matters is how the economic agents make their decisions regarding the holdings of their real balances. Empirical research has been directed to demonstrate that, in fact, the demand for money is stable. This stability is crucial for assessing the impact of higher/lower real balances on aggregate spending and on the balance of payments. In Keynesian theory, any impact on aggregate spending (real decisions) from an increase in the money supply is mediated through the rate of interest. In monetarist analysis, such impact is directly transmitted to aggregate spending because money is an asset, and any increase in it is likely to result in unwanted money holdings that yield a lower rate of return on the total asset portfolio. The public, then, finds itself with unwanted real balances that have to be disposed of by acquiring other assets with higher yields, thus effecting a portfolio adjustment. In the particular case of an increase in money supply over the desired real balances, the unwanted real balances could be disposed of by buying foreign goods and services, thus creating deficits in the balance of payments.

The demand for real balances is satisfied by the money supply which is a multiple of the money base. The latter has two components: the domestic credit creation and the international reserves. Now, if the assumptions listed above hold true, the existence of deficits or surpluses in the balance of payments and the mechanism to eliminate them can be explained as follows:

Under fixed exchange rates, the money supply is endogenously determined. What this means is that the power of monetary policy is all but eliminated since the government cannot control total money supply. This fact denotes a fundamental difference from the stabilization policies of the 1950s where inflationary pressures were tackled through monetary restraint. In the monetary approach to the balance of payments, changes in the domestic credit component of the money supply are offset in equal magnitude by changes in the international reserves. The latter is seen as adjusting passively to the changes induced by the former and constitute the deficit or surplus in the balance of payments.

Now, deficits or surpluses exist whenever there is disequilibrium in the money market, i.e., when there is a divergence between money supply and the demand for money. For example, a balance of payments deficit reflects an excess supply of domestic credit that in turn produces an excess demand for goods and services, since the economic agents wish to dispose of unwanted real balances by increasing total imports and by investing abroad. Likewise, a surplus in the balance of payments reflects an excess demand for money, which, provided that the domestic credit is not increased by the monetary authority, has to be satisfied by an increase of international reserves in the form of additional inflow of foreign capital, which ultimately leads to an expansion in the money supply.

What is of particular importance is the fact that the monetary approach to the balance of payments predicts that any deficit or surplus is likely to be eliminated by a self-correcting mechanism provided that the monetary authorities do not hamper the movement of monetary flows. The important consequence of this is that there is a tendency toward long-run equilibrium in the balance of payments in which "the money market must be in full stock equilibrium, otherwise the portfolio of assets would be continually changing, thus inducing changes in the flow of expenditures."(10) To clarify, let us consider again the case of a deficit in the balance of payments, which, as stated above, reflects an excess demand for goods and services. As long as the monetary authorities do not intervene by expanding domestic money supply, there will be a decrease in the money supply thus bringing it to the level associated with wanted real balances and restoring equilibrium in the money market. With no government intervention, this decrease in the money supply will come--of course--in the form of a fall in the level of international reserves.

The consequences of what has been cited above are far-reaching. According to this theory, it is not difficult to see that government authorities can do very little to prevent the balance of payments from reaching equilibrium, or in other words from maintaining deficits or surpluses. Persistent deficits, for example, are directly caused by government intervention since the roots of the latter are to be traced exclusively to the expansion of domestic credit above the real balances that the economic agents really want. Therefore, it is not surprising that, in the Peruvian case, monetarist analysis attributes the cause of external crisis to the pressures on the balance of payments brought about by an excessive domestic credit mainly channeled to the public sector.(11)

At this point, given the self-correcting adjustment mechanism that the monetary approach postulates, it is proper to ask whether a devaluation of the exchange rate has a role to play. In order to answer this, let us first examine the effects of devaluation for the monetary approach.

A devaluation of the exchange rate will immediately raise the price level, stemming from a direct price increase of products tied to the world market (imports and exports), and, to a lesser degree, from a rise in the prices of products for the domestic market. The increase in the price level means that the real balances that people hold have declined <u>relatively</u> to the balances they would like to hold, in other words, economic agents exert, in fact, a higher demand for money. They can restore the desired level of real balances by satisfying their higher demand for money from international sources thus bringing on an inflow of foreign capital, or by cutting aggregate spending. In both cases, the consequences are likely to be the elimination of the deficit and even the appearance of a surplus. The important point in the mechanism of devaluation is that the government authorities should not expand domestic credit following devaluation since this will force the public to satisfy their demand for money from abroad.

Therefore, the impact on the balance of payments operates only through the money market. But if disequilibrium in the balance of payments is self-correcting, of what use is devaluation? The answer is that it cannot be useful in the long-run. However, in the short-run, it is a good instrument which accelerates the process by which equilibrium in the balance of payments is restored, that is, by inducing a decline in aggregate spending. Also, since devaluation as indicated above induces an increase in the price level, this effect being stronger in tradeable goods, it is expected that there will be an internal shift in resources in favor of production of these goods with relatively less incentive to increase production of the nontradeable goods. Nevertheless, the core of this approach is that, given some time, devaluation or any other policies affecting real expenditures are unnecessary because the self-correcting mechanism leads to equilibrium in the long-run. Despite the appeal of this tenet, however, advocates of this doctrine cannot come up with a precise definition of "some time." Also, Keynes' famous dictum "in the long-run we are all dead" is in my opinion still disturbingly appealing.

For all its theoretical strength, the monetary approach to the balance of payments presents some weaknesses which are of particular relevance for the economies of less developed countries. I will discuss two:

1. The lumping together of the familiar components of the balance of payments is particularly disturbing insofar as the differing characteristics of the external accounts are blurred. The importance of this should not be underestimated, especially in light of analysis of political economy. By this I imply the necessary recognition of the difference between the current account and the capital account. By analyzing the former, it is possible to obtain a good insight regarding the relative strength of the productive sector whose dynamics are tied to the international markets and which, as repeatedly stated, provides the most dynamic source for growth. On the other hand, a glance at the capital account will give an idea about the composition of capital inflows (public and private), how they are appropriated internally, and how its balance fluctuates. In less developed

countries, movements in this account have taken on a tremendous importance for their financial health since the 1970s, and it is not at all possible to provide an analysis of this account devoid of political considerations. Below I shall mention two "pure" economic reasons of why neglect of this account may lead to overlooking important contemporary features in the balance of payments.

The first has to do with the massive increase in foreign debt that has occurred in many less-developed countries as a result of the quadrupling of the oil prices or as a result of conscious borrowing to finance investment projects. In general terms, the latter was the case of Peru. A very serious complication could arise if the increase in foreign debt is in the form of inflows of short-term loans while at the same time the country faces huge deficits in the current account. In fact, this was the situation facing Peru in the mid-1970s. The nature of the debt, the repayment terms, the changing conditions in the international money markets, and the very sizeable deficit in the current account led to the situation with which we are now familiar: the quick loss of the country's reserves and the beginning of the stabilization programs.

The second reason is indirectly associated with the first, at least in its origin. Essentially, as Carlos Díaz Alejandro argues,(12) the late 1970s were characterized by a dramatic increase in the interest elasticity of the international supply of financial funds. What this means is that there has been an increase in capital mobility and thus a closer linkage between domestic and international capital markets. The experiences of Argentina and Chile in the late 1970s are not unimportant. The economic consequence of this is that the authorities have lesser discretionary power over their monetary policies. Generally, an increase in the inflow of foreign capital will raise the money supply and this, under fixed exchange rates, will lead to the appreciation of the local currency. Given an exchange-rate-elasticity of exports, this could hamper the competitive position of the export sector and set off pressures to devalue the currency. Díaz Alejandro's point, however, is Keynesian in spirit and as such is quickly dismissed by monetarists on theoretical grounds. For monetarists a rise in the local rate of interest, ceteris paribus, will in the end produce an external deficit because the opportunity cost of holding money will be higher, thus inducing a situation in which the demand for money is lowered.(13)

2. The other disturbing feature of the monetary approach to the balance of payments that I would like to point out is the unrelenting faith it places in the power and effectiveness of the market mechanism to bring about long-run equilibrium in all markets at levels of full employment of resources. This implies the belief in the non-rigidity of wages and prices and also the idea that government intervention in the economic life of a society becomes unnecesary. All to the contrary, government fiscal and monetary policy aimed at affecting aggregate demand in the long-run hampers the market mechanism and thus reduces welfare.

Therefore, it is not unreasonable to argue that a good deal of this approach owes its theoretical content to the classical postulates which prevailed before the Keynesian revolution. For example, a deficit in the balance of payments was depicted as a situation in which outpayments exceeded inpayments measured in foreign currency. In other words, what prevails is a situation in which the demand for foreign currency exceeds the supply. Equilibrium in the balance of payments would be restored by market forces as long as the government did not intervene with fiscal and monetary policies aimed at stimulating economic activity. Thus, a balance of payments deficit, ceteris paribus, leads to a decrease in the domestic money supply. This in turn leads to a fall in consumption, investment, and consequently in the level of income and employment. Also, it is expected that a lower domestic money supply will lead to lower price levels. The combination of these effects--lower income and lower price levels--leads to the reduction of the level of imports and, through the greater competitiveness of the country's products, to an increase in the level of exports. Therefore, the system had a self-correcting mechanism that ensured the elimination of the deficit.

It can be seen, therefore, that in the classical world, deflating the economy was the way to restore equilibrium in the external sector. Of course, this is a recipe for a situation in which there exists excessive aggregate demand. What is remarkably interesting is how twentieth century stabilization policies, especially those applied in the 1970s in Chile, Argentina, and Peru, have consistently resorted to this diagnosis and thus have consistently advocated deflationary policies to ride out the crisis. Deflationary policies, in this sense, are to be understood as the conscious government intervention to make the market mechanism work, i.e., the lifting of controls that prevented equilibrium between supply and demand. Of this, more will be said in the last chapter. At this point, however, I do want to stress the analytical association existing between the stabilization policies and the classical postulates which placed so much faith in the virtues of the free market mechanism. As such, it is very difficult to ignore the case of Chile in the 1970s. What critics and defenders alike labeled "shock treatment" was nothing but the too rigorous, conscious application of deflationary policies.

Applicability

In light of the theoretical rationale of the stabilization policies that has just been discussed, let us briefly provide some insights aimed at questioning the appropriateness of these policies for the Peruvian case.

First there is the problem of "theory ladenness." What this concept refers to is the tendency in social sciences to observe reality through all the concepts that have been embedded in the theory beforehand. The consequence of this is the manipulation of the subject matter to mirror the theory and, therefore, the loss of any real hope of objectivity.

Economics is not devoid of this problem, as has been evidenced by the diagnoses of the Peruvian crisis. In the specific case of the monetary approach to the balance of payments, which has greatly influenced officials of the International Monetary Fund and Peruvian Central Bankers alike, its analysis invariably leads to pointing out excess demand as the root of the crisis. This view, however, has been sharply criticized by Schydlowsky, as was discussed in the introduction, and also by Thorp, Boloña, and Herzka, who assert that the observed increase in public investment "was not inflationary because it was far outweighed by, and partly responsible for, the very large increase in the external deficit, the deflationary effect of which outweighed all other factors in those years" (1974 and 1975).(14) Thus, they attribute the inflation rates of 17 percent in 1974 and 25 percent in 1975 not to excess demand but rather to the increase in the price of imports.

The appropriateness of the stabilization policies could be also judged by examining the validity of the theoretical assumptions that underlie the application of these policies. For example, in the specific case of the monetary approach to the balance of payments, the assumption of perfect capital mobility should ensure the equalization of the local rate of interest with that rate prevaling in the international markets (given that the economy is small vis-à-vis the rest of the world). In Peru, after being fixed for over sixty years, the rate of interest was "liberalized" in the period of 1977-1978. Despite that the government raised the local interest rate at a level substantially higher than the foreign rates, there was actually no attraction of short- and long-term capital; as will be revealed in the next chapter, recovery in the external sector was entirely induced by the reversal of the deficit in the current account. This phenomenon is strikingly different from the Chilean experience, for example. In this country, there was a massive influx of foreign capital during the stabilization period; however, the local rate of interest was never equalized with the foreign rates, reflecting, in all likelihood, a local financial market that has an oligopolistic structure.

Finally, let us consider the policy which is of the most interest for this study: devaluation. The approaches that have been discussed above portray the virtues of this policy, especially as a short-term instrument which should restore equilibrium in the external sector and which should increase real ouput and employment. As a result, orthodoxy rejects hidden forms of devaluation, such as the ones which would restrict trade: tariffs, quantitative restrictions on imports, restrictions on foreign exchange use, export taxes, etc., on the grounds that these impair the effectiveness of the market mechanism and thus lead to misallocation of resources. However, as Taylor and Krugman argue,(15) there seems to be some justification in the resistance of less developed countries (among them Peru) to devaluate their currency when they confront the structural characteristics and the likely social, economic, and political effects of devaluation. In the Peruvian case, there seems to be a well justified case for elasticity pessimism, both on imports and exports. In the case of imports, Thorp, Boloña and Herzka cite an empirical study made by Pirani in 1977 which shows that the demand for imports is insensitive to price.(16) Also, given the fact that the bulk of Peruvian

exports still depends on primary products, rapid production
response to more favorable international prices is constrained by
available capacity; it is likely, therefore, that exports are
supply inelastic. As a final point, devaluation is likely to
induce speculative effects and a regressive income distribution.
Considerable space will be devoted to this in the next chapter.

48

NOTES

[1]This survey is based on Cabrera, op.cit., and Thorp, Boloña, and Herzka, op.cit., where a detailed description is provided.

[2]R. Campos, "Monetarism and Structuralism in Latin America", in Gerald M. Meier, Leading Issues in Economic Development. 3rd. ed. (New York: Oxford University Press, 1976), pp. 316-321.

[3]Lance Taylor, "IS/LM in the Tropics", in Cline and Weintraub, op.cit., p.471

[4]This discussion has benefited from the work of Thomas F. Dernburg and Duncan M. McDougall, Macroeconomics. 5th ed. (McGraw-Hill, Inc., 1976).

[5]Harry Johnson, "Elasticity, Absorption, Keynesian Multiplier, Keynesian Policy, and Monetary Approaches to Devaluation", American Economic Review 66 (1976), 450.

[6]This discussion has greatly benefitted from the work of Alejandro Foxley, Experimentos Neoliberales en América Latina (Santiago, Chile: Colección Estudios CIEPLAN, 7 No.59, 1982).

[7]This discussion is based on Howard R. Vane & Joyn L. Thomson, Monetarism: Theory, Evidence and Practice (Oxford: Martin Robertson, 1980), and on Mordechai E. Kreinin and Lawrence H. Officer, The Monetary Approach to the Balance of Payments: A Survey, Princeton Studies in International Finance No. 43, 1978.

[8]Mordechai E. Kreinin, International Economics: A Policy Approach. 3rd. ed. (New York: Harcourt Brace Jovanovic, 1979), p. 138.

[9]Vane and Thomson, op.cit., p.168.

[10]Ibid., 171.

[11]Jorge González Izquierdo, Perú: Una Economía en Crisis. Interpretación y Bases para una Solución. 4th. ed. (Lima, Peru: Universidad del Pacifico, Centro de Investigación, 1980), p. 190.

[12]Carlos Díaz Alejandro, "Southern Cone Stabilization Plans" (Yale University: Economic Growth Center, Paper No.330, 1979), p.16.

[13]Kreinin, op.cit., p. 149.

[14]Thorp, Boloña, and Herzka, op.cit., p. 25.

[15]Taylor and Krugman. op.cit., 450.

[16]Thorp, Boloña, and Herzka, op.cit., p.46.

IV
Devaluation: Empirical Results
and Macroeconomic Impact

It should be clear by now, as demonstrated in the last chapter, that exchange-rate adjustment plays a significant role in orthodox stabilization policies. From this point, the study will address itself toward exploring devaluation-induced results that run opposite to the standard corollaries that neo-classical theory implies. In other words, the model which was presented in the first chapter is aimed at demonstrating that an increase in domestic output which should result from more efficient resource allocation (in the direction of production of exportables and import-substituting goods) is not likely to occur when some vital, structural features of semi-industrialized economies are incorporated into the analysis and, fundamentally, when the significant income effects are taken into consideration. By the latter, what is implied is the recognition that devaluation alters the income shares of social groups and thus directly affects aggregate demand.

Therefore, the purpose of this chapter is to test the basic theoretical postulates which have been outlined in the previous chapters, and as such, it constitutes the core of the study. To carry out these tests, I shall deal first with the theoretical rationale that underlies the model and its association or disassociation with Peruvian reality will be pointed out immediately. Second, I will analyze the basic structure of the model applied to the Peruvian experience of 1975 and thus evaluate the reasonableness of its parameters by comparing them with other studies. Finally I will perform the empirical simulations for the three years which cover the stabilization period and contrast the results with the actual aggregate indicators to assess its predictive ability and therefore lay the ground work for an overall evaluation of the macroeconomic impact of devaluation.

Theoretical Rationale

Taylor acknowledges that the construction of the model is based upon the theoretical framework contributed by Michael Kalecki.(1) Its fundamental concepts and focus of study depart from neoclassical economics. Rather it is associated primarily with the Cambridge (England) School of Economics. Of the various

issues that separate this school from the neoclassical counterpart, two are especially relevant to this study: the microeconomic
base and the distributional effects. The latter will be explored
first.(2)

As opposed to neoclassical economics, income distribution is
not endogenously determined in the production process by the
contribution that every input provides at the margin. Instead,
income distribution responds to institutional and historical
factors that have conditioned and limited the distribution shares
between workers and owners of the means of production before the
production process takes place. In a journey back to the classical paradigm, the division of income that society generates is
between a non-residual share, which belongs to the non-property
owners and a residual share which belongs to the property owners
(of the means of production). The relative changes of shares are
in turn determined by the nature of the economic cycle or, in
other words, by the rate of economic expansion (investment) which
by definition is controlled by the property owners. It is
further assumed that the non-property owners spend all or most of
their non-residual income on consumption, thus leaving virtually
nothing for savings.

Turning now to the microeconomic base, a crucial assumption
dividing the Kaleckian framework from the neoclassical is the
explicit recognition of the existence of imperfect markets with
some degree of monopoly. Price determination will therefore rest
upon conditions on the supply side and not on the free interplay
of supply and demand which a Walrasian-type general equilibrium
model would imply. In the Kaleckian framework, demand only
determines the volume of production but any demand shift has no
impact over price since the firm faces a roughly constant average
cost curve over the relevant range of output. In these circumstances, profits are positively related to the rate of capacity
utilization (itself determined by demand) because an expanding
output vis-à-vis a constant variable (prime) costs and a fixed
price means that the average total cost per unit must be falling
over the relevant range of output.

It should be clear from these considerations that in the
Kaleckian world the pricing decisions respond entirely to conditions only on the supply side since demand variations exert no
pressures on costs. This pricing model is based on mark-up above
costs. What determines the size of the mark-up according to
Kalecki is the "degree of monopoly" or the expected rate of
capacity utilization. What is important to bear in mind is that
the size of the mark-up will actually constitute the bulk of
internal savings of the economy and, as such, are generated and
appropriated by the oligopolies. Any measurement of the internal
savings of the economy should therefore be directed at examining
the retained earnings of these corporations.

At this point I would like to enrich this theoretical discussion by gradually incorporating well-accepted features of Peruvian reality along with some stylized facts and implicit assumptions of the simulation model already outlined in the first
chapter. Since this task is reasonably complicated, I shall
proceed gradually.

1. As stated in the introduction, the division of national income among two social groups is, in fact, arbitrary when one is confronted with the nature of Peruvian society where the so-called informal sector is of no small importance insofar as the independent workers (small craftsmen, street vendors, civil service workers, etc.) who make up this sector draw approximately 22 percent of national income. For the purposes of this study, this sector has been grouped in with labor in order to be faithful to theoretical consistency. In fact, as might be recalled, implicit in the Kaleckian framework is the idea that property owners' income, which is residual, contains the bulk of savings. If it is assumed that property owners reinvest or retain all their income, it means that their marginal propensity to save is one. Therefore, what is crucially important in determining into which income class the informal sector should be incorporated is the ability of this sector to generate a residual income, savings, or retained earnings which constitute endogenous sources for investment. A study carried out by the Instituto Nacional de Planificación, however, shows that such ability is non-existent since it demonstrates empirically that the informal sector's marginal propensity to consume is 0.978.(3) It should be noted, however, that this study provides no information on the methodological procedure for obtaining the level of aggregation of this sector.

2. The model explicitly assumes a two-sector economy, one producing exportables and importables (traded goods) the other producing for the internal, home market (non-traded goods). This division of the Peruvian economy is a good starting point to unveil the structural mechanisms which exert so much influence over one of the most critical variables that typically affect less-developed countries: the rate of investment. With respect to the sector producing for internal demand, the highly concentrated structure of its most dynamic element--the manufacturing industry--implies an oligopolistic market that practices mark-up pricing. In the second chapter it was pointed out that investment in the manufacturing sector has been directed towards the utilization of labor-saving techniques. It was also stated how this sector is characterized by the existence of idle capacity; therefore, the supply schedule of home goods is likely to present a high elasticity.

3. With regard to the external sector, it is assumed that both exports and imports are price-inelastic in the short-run. This elasticity pessimism seems to be well-founded in the Peruvian case, since the bulk of its exports--well into the mid-1970s--were traditional products, as was pointed out in the second chapter. Rather than price, the volume of exports would depend mainly on available capacity. In the case of imports, it was pointed out in the last chapter that they are not sensitive to price changes. As previously shown, the bulk of these imports are concentrated in raw materials and semi-fabricated goods which are vital inputs for the industrial sector and which are not easily substituted in the short-run. (See Table 4.)

With all this in mind, let us spell out the mechanism for which devaluation might produce a fall in domestic output.(4)

In order to do so, I shall highlight two main features which underlie the model:

1. What is crucially important in the recognition of two different income groups is that they have different marginal propensities to save. The income of labor is determined by the real wage, which is strongly related to the rate of investment but which in nominal terms responds to institutional factors such as union pressures. Most, if not all, of this labor income is devoted to consumption. As a result the marginal propensity of this group to save has to be lower than that of the property owners.

2. It could be argued further that both groups have different patterns of consumption. In fact it is not unreasonable to assume that Peruvian groups of high incomes prefer imported goods (as consumers) to home-made goods. As expected, the other element of their expenditures, investment, has been tied to imports of capital goods.

Now, a decision to devaluate the exchange rate will immediately cause a relative price effect. The prices of the traded goods (exportables and importables) will rise relatively to the prices of non-traded goods (goods for the home market). The shift in relative prices should encourage production of exportables and import substituting goods since their profitability should be relatively higher, and therefore, through reallocation of resources, total output should increase. As previously noted, the rationale of such policy takes on greater importance in the presence of idle resources.

Unfortunately, the situation is not that simple when income effects are incorporated into the analysis. First of all, it is imperative to recognize that devaluation will raise the price of non-traded goods since most of them have a high import component. If it is further assumed that wages remain constant in the short-run, or at best do not keep up with the cost of living index, a drop in real wages is inevitable. Second, with a given world price the prices of exportables rise in domestic terms, assuming that the supply of them is inelastic. In any case, what is certain to happen is that the property owners in the export sector are likely to benefit from windfall profits, whether or not there is an increase in export supply.

It should be pointed out that this is a somewhat simplified version of actual economic reality in the sense that this analysis ignores imported inputs that might be needed by the export sector. Nevertheless, I argue that this last consideration should in no way alter the fact that windfall profits are expected in the export sector. Specifically, in the Peruvian case, given the nature of the export sector, it is safe to assume that imported inputs are not that important, because, in the case of traditional exports (minerals, sugar, fish, etc.), the relative importance of imports needed for operations is likely to be strongly felt in start-up costs which require the purchase of costly capital goods and equipment. For example, once a mine is in operation, it is highly likely that the need for imported goods will decrease significantly, although the purchase of spare parts and salaries of foreign personnel may continue or rise. On the other hand, whatever potential exists in Peru for non-traditional exports, their success depends on the heavy use of the most abundant local input: in this case, labor.

It is safe to assume therefore that whatever the technical conditions of production in the export sector, there will be an increase in the profit margins which will be reaped by the property owners. This redistribution of income is likely to have adverse effects on the output of home-industry goods (the non-traded) sector. In fact, what takes place is an income redistribution in favor of the group which has a higher marginal propensity to save. In other words, the greater the fall in the relative income share of that group which has a high marginal propensity to consume home goods (non-property owners), the larger will be the drop in the output of these goods. The fall in output following a devaluation, therefore, will take the form of an excess supply of home goods, since there has been a fall in aggregate demand. This result will be aggravated if the property owners do not channel increasing savings into higher consumption of home-produced goods whose prices are now relatively cheaper; in other words, if the cross elasticity of demand for home goods with respect to the price of traded goods is negligible. As noted before, low cross elasticity of demand is most likely to be the case in a country such as Peru, where foreign-induced demonstration effects cater their consumption and investment decisions in favor of imported goods.

The only way to avoid these negative results is for the economy to rapidly take advantage of the favorable conditions arising in the traded sector as a consequence of devaluation. Basically, what this means is that the ability to expand the supply of exports rapidly should be present. Regardless of the nature of the export products and their associated demand elasticities, such ability will depend on the combination of internal and external factors, which greatly limit and condition a positive response by exports. Suffice it to say for the moment that, in the Peruvian case, such ability is constrained by the existing available productive capacity in traditional exports. On the other hand, it is also safe to assume that the possibilities of substituting locally-produced inputs for imported inputs are limited in the short-run due to the complexity of production techniques.

Before bringing this discussion to a close, it should be indicated that theoretically another way exists to address the likelihood of negative-output effects of devaluation in the context of a semi-industrialized economy. Such a theoretical framework has been provided by Lance Taylor in his article "IS/LM in the Tropics: Diagramatics of the New Structural Macro Critique."(5) Again, at heart, the framework is Kaleckian in spirit and it is enriched through the use of Keynesian-Hicksian tools (shapes of IS and LM curves adapted to structural features in less developed countries) to describe the likelihood of stag-flation as a result of the application of typical stabilization policies (monetary contraction, fiscal discipline, and devaluation). A basic premise is that interest costs are part of production costs, thus any changes in the former should have an effect on final price, which is fixed by mark-up. As a result, in the aggregate, the price level will not be independent of the rate of interest since they are positively correlated. This permits output to be related directly to the price level. In the particular case of devaluation, according to Taylor's presentation, the LM curve is likely to shift to the left since a higher demand for money is needed to sustain production because imports are now relatively more expensive. Even if exports respond positively, if the shape of the LM curve is very steep, in the short run it is likely that the result will be a contraction in output with a rise in the price level.

At this point, the inner logic of the theoretical model should be clear. The immediate task to be performed, therefore, is to relate the model to the Peruvian economic structure. In other words, the task ahead is to solve the values of the input-output coefficients by using national accounts as raw data and by checking their reasonableness as an approximation of values which have been derived from other studies. This is an essential task, for it will provide the input for the empirical simulations which are to be performed next. I shall turn now to the analysis of the structure.

Structure

In this section, I shall first develop an initial, basic solution of the entire model for which the values of the parameters obtained will be used to predict the actual trends of the national output during the years of stabilization. The methodology to be used has been suggested by Lance Taylor and employed in an empirical case study of Portugal(6) and by Stephen E. Guisinguer in his analysis of stabilization policies in Pakistan.(7)

For the purpose of this study, 1975 has been selected as a base year. The values of the variables utilized to work out the basic solution are shown in Table 8.

In order to obtain a solution for the values of the coefficients of the model, let us assume that the price of the home goods (P_H), the price of exports (P_X), the world price of exports ($P*_X$), the price of imports (P_M), the world price of imports ($P*_M$), the exchange rate (e), and the wage rate (w) are all equal to unity. Let us further assume that ad-valorem taxes on exports and imports are equal to zero. Therefore:

$$P_H = P_X = P*_X = P_M = P*_M = e = w = 1$$
$$tm = tx = 0$$

With all these assumptions in mind, the solution will be derived as follows:

1. Total Home-Goods Output Cost

By definition, it is the product of home goods output (X_H) times its price (P_H).

From equation No.1 in the introduction, let
$$(a_{LH}w + a_{MH}P_M) = B_H \text{ , so}$$
$$P_H X_H = B_H (1+Z)X_H + B_H(1 + Z)X_H V_H$$

TABLE 8

VARIABLES ENTERING THE BASIC SOLUTION
(Values for 1975)

==

A. Components of Gross Domestic Product (in current millions of soles)

Consumption (C)	476,752
Government Expenditure (G)	81,752
Investment (I)	123,159
Exports (X)	67,980
Imports (M)	122,251
Gross Domestic Product (GDP)	627,392
Indirect Taxes (T)	57,169
Home goods output (X_H)	
C + I + G	681,663

B. National Income Shares

	Amount (Current millions of soles)	Percentage
1. Non-property owners share		
Wages and salaries	230,061	41.12
Independent workers	119,308	21.84
Total	349,369	63.96
2. Property owners share		
Rent	17,498	3.20
Net interest	5,268	.96
Gross profits	174,021	31.86
Total	196,787	36.02

C. Taxes

	Amount (Current millions of soles)
1. On labor income	
Subsidies	12,655
Payroll taxes	2,596
2. On profit income	
Direct taxes	25,994
Payroll taxes	3,656

Source: INE, Cuentas Nacionales del Perú 1950-1980.

We want to solve first for V_H, so by substituting and rearranging:

$$-B_H(1 + Z) \ X_H = P_H X_H + B_H(1 + Z) X_H V_H$$

$$B_H(1 + Z) \ (681,663) = 1(681,663) \ (57,169)$$

$$B_H(1 + Z) = \frac{681,663 - 57,169}{681,663}$$

$$B_H(1 + Z) = 0.9161$$

$$V_H = (\frac{1}{(0.9161)}) \ 1 \ = 0.0916$$

To arrive at a solution for the value of the input coefficient of imports into home-goods (a_{MH}), it is assumed that the total import bill is entirely used as intermediate inputs into home-goods production. In the Peruvian case, this is a valid assumption, since, as the analysis of the external sector demonstrated in Chapter II, the amount of imports going for final demand is negligible. In fact, as can be seen in Table 4, the bulk of imports is made up of capital goods and semi-processed products. Therefore:

$$a_{MH} = \frac{M}{X_H}$$

$$a_{MH} = \frac{122251}{681663}$$

$$a_{MH} = .1793$$

The reasonableness of the value of this coefficient as an approximation of reality is demonstrated by the fact that the estimated a_{MH}, when combined with the input coefficient of labor into home-goods (a_{LH}) and which is to be calculated below, shows that imports constitute 28 percent of all inputs in the manufacting sector. This percentage is contrasted with other empirical studies which show that share to be approximately 33 percent.[8] Since this approximation is reasonably close, I conclude that the value of 0.1793 for a_{MH} is reasonable.

To obtain the value of the input coefficient of labor into home-goods (a_{LH}), let us first calculate value added at factor cost (VAFC):

$$VAFC = X_H - T - M = 681663 - 57169 - 122251 = 502203$$

The labor share of national income is 63.96 percent (see Table 8). The reason why it is assumed that the independent workers are included in the total labor income share has already been stated at the beginning of this chapter, in the previous section. Now, it is possible to find a_{LH} by applying the following formula:

$$a_{LH} = \frac{\text{Labor income share (VAFC)}}{X_H}$$

$$a_{LH} = \frac{(0.6396)(502243)}{(681663)}$$

$$a_{LH} = .4713$$

At this point, solutions have been found for all the values of the parameters that are included in the equation for the price of home goods except the mark-up factor Z. This value can be obtained by substitution:

$$P_H = (a_{LH}w + a_{MH}P_M)(1 + Z)(1 + V_H)$$
$$1 = [.4713(1) + .1793(1)](1 + Z)(1 + 0.0916)$$
$$Z = .4081$$

Again, it is possible to test the accuracy or the approximation of the size of the mark-up by comparing it with some other estimates derived in other empirical studies. As such, in a study related to three representative sectors of the Peruvian industry (food, chemicals, and electric machinery), Miguel Bacharach has found that the size of the mark-ups for the three sectors are .37, .50, and .56 respectively.(9) I conclude, therefore, that a value of 0.4081 for Z is a reasonable approximation.

2. Income Shares

To calculate the wage and profit share, I shall proceed piecemeal. Let us take up the former first.

The wage or labor share consists of income derived from the home-goods industry, income generated in the export industry, and taxes on income which are subtracted. In the case of Peru, income taxes on labor income are virtually non-existent; on the contrary, what exist are government subsidies which, by definition, have to be added to the labor income. Therefore:

a) Home goods income
.4713 (681663) = 321268
b) Exports income = Total wage income (wages and salaries plus income of independent workers -home-goods income)
= 230061 + 119308 - 321268 = 28101, which is 41.34 percent of total export income.
c) Subsidies 12655

Therefore, total wage income (Yw) = 321268 + 28101 + 12655 =362024

Likewise, the profit share, which is a residual, can be calculated by adding the proceeds originated in the home-goods industry plus the ones derived from the export industry. To this, one has to add the remittances from nationals working abroad. In the Peruvian case, this is a negative flow, implying that from the total profits proceeds one has to subtract a given amount (originated either in home goods or in the export sector) which is sent abroad. Perhaps the most accurate name that can be applied to this phenomenon is capital flight. In 1975, that amount was -8687.

To calculate the total profit share,
   a) From home-goods = VAFC-labor income
                   502243 - 321268 = 180975
   b) From exports = (100 - % labor share) (X)
                   (100-41.34)(67980) = 39877
   c) Remittances = 8687

Therefore, the total profit income (Y_R)= 180975+39877-8687 = 212165

3. Consumption Expenditures

The goal here is to calculate the marginal propensities of workers and property owners to consume. With regard to the former, the simulation performed by the Instituto Nacional de Planificación in 1973 gives a 0.998 of marginal propensity to consume for wage income and 0.978 of the same for income of independent workers.(10) For the purposes of this study, an overall marginal propensity to consume of 0.99 will be assumed for the entire non-property-owning group. Total consumption expenditure of this group is obtained by multiplying 0.99 times total labor income. Previously, one has to subtract from it the payroll taxes (see Table 8). Therefore:

$$Dw = dw (Yw - Tw)$$
$$Dw = 0.99 (362024 - 2596) = 355884$$

Now, the property owners' consumption expenditure is obtained in the same manner. Again, the main goal is to calculate d_r (marginal propensity of property owners to consume). To obtain it, let us first calculate

$$D_R = d_r (Y_R - T_R)$$

The value of Y_R is already known. Direct taxes in Peru are entirely applied to property owners and in 1975 these amounted to S/. 25994. (See Table 8.)

To this one has to add some payroll taxes imputed to employers and which are not recorded as indirect taxes. The total amount of these was S/. 3656. (See Table 8.) So,

$$T_R = 25994 + 3656 = 29650$$

And,
$$D_R = d_r (212165 - 29650)$$
$$D_R = d_r (182515)$$

However, D_R could be calculated as a residual (value of total consumption less consumption expenditure of non-property owners). Thus,

$$D_R = 476752 - 355884 = 120918$$
$$d_r = D_R/Y_R - T_R$$

$d_r = \dfrac{120918}{182515}$

$d_r = 0.6625$

Once again, the reasonableness of this last estimate can be tested by comparing it with other empirical studies. In 1968, Eugene Brady published "A Methodological Procedure for Analyzing the Policy Instruments of an Underdeveloped Economy - Using the Economy of Peru as a Demonstrative Case", where he shows empirically that the value of d_r after taxes is 0.6339.(11) For this reason, our estimate is reasonably precise.

The methodology that has been used so far to estimate the main parameters can be further put to the test by checking its consistency with the Savings - Investment identity (equation 13 of the model).

Accordingly,

$$P_H I = S_{PRIV} + S_{GOV} + S_{FOR}$$

Therefore, let us derive a solution for each type of savings:

$$S_{PRIV} = (1-dw)(Y_w-T_w)+(1-d_r)(Y_R-T_R)$$

$$(1-.99)(362204-2596)+(1-0.6625)(182515)= 65197$$

$$S_{GOV}=V_H P_H X_H/(1+V_H)+et_x P^*_x X+et_M P^* a_{MH} X_H+T_w+T_R-P_H G=$$

$$.0916(1)(681663)/(1+0.0916)+0+0-10059+29650+81752 = -4962$$

$$S_{FOR} = eP_M^* a_{MH} X_H - eP_X^* X - e(REM)$$

$$= 1(1)(.1793)(681663)-1(1)(67890)-1(8687) = 62929$$

So, $P_H I = 65197 - 4962 + 62929 = 123164$

which, compared with what the national accounts show for the value of investment (123159) is such a small difference as to be immaterial, for all intents and purposes.

4.   The Multiplier

First let us derive a solution for Q. Accordingly,

$$Q= 1-dwa_{LH}\frac{w}{P_H} - d_r \frac{z}{(1+Z)(1+V_H)}$$

$$= 1 - 0.99 (0.4713) (1/1)-0.6625 \frac{0.4081}{(1.4081)(1.0916)}$$

$$= 0.3575$$

So, the multiplier is:

$$1/Q = 1/0.3575$$

$$= 2.7970$$

Finally, all the values needed to derive the solution for the main variable of the entire model, which is home-goods output (X_H), have been obtained. Accordingly,

$$X_H = (1/Q)\{(X/P_H)\,[(d_w - d_r)a_{LX}w + d_r P_X] + (1/P_H)\,[d_r e(REM) - (d_w T_w + d_r T_R)] + I + G\}$$

$= 2.7970 \ (67980/1)\,[(.99 - .6625)(.4134)(1) + .6625(1)] +$
$[.6625(1)(-8687) - (.99)\ (-10059) + .6625(29650)] + 123159 \ + 81752$
$= 2.7970(5421 + 189471)$
$X_H = 681663,$

which is the same value of home-goods output (C + I + G).

As should be remembered, the purpose of this methodological discourse was to provide the value of the main parameters of the model. Not only does their accuracy prove to be reasonable when compared with other estimates, but their inclusion within macro relationships was consistent in the sense that the entire exercise satisfies national account identities. By using the values just derived and the raw data provided by the National Accounts, it is possible to test the model to assess how well it predicts actual experience. To do so, the technique to be used is empirical simulation. This exercise will be the substance of the next section.

Results

Empirical simulations were carried out for the periods 1975-1976, 1976-1977, and 1977-1978. The goal was to predict the fluctuations of home-goods output (C + I + G) or what is also called total absorption and the shifts in income distribution for those three periods. The results are to be compared with the actual data. At the same time, the simulation program should provide: data for the gross national product at nominal and pre-devaluation factor cost; an estimate of the price of home goods, which could be used as a good approximation for a comparison with the consumer price index; estimates of import and export prices indices; and an estimate of the variation of the real wage rate.

The data, as stated previously, come from two sources:

1. The values of the parameters estimated in the last section which are to remain fixed since this study is limited by short-run analysis.

2. The components of gross domestic product which are obtained directly from the National Accounts. They are shown in Table 9.

TABLE 9

EMPIRICAL SIMULATIONS:MAJOR COMPONENTS
OF GROSS DOMESTIC PRODUCT
(in current millions of soles)

	Period 1975-1976	Period 1976-1977	Period 1977-1978
Consumption	476,752	621,500	851,700
Government expenditure	81,752	107,800	168,500
Investment	123,159	150,100	171,400
Trade balance	-54,271	-49,000	48,400
Gross domestic product	627,392	830,400	1,143,000
Indirect taxes	57,169	77,023	113,524
Home-goods output (X_H)	681,663	879,400	1,191,600

Source: INE, Cuentas Nacionales del Perú 1950-1980.

Let us now state the values of the parameters which will be constant:

$$a_{LH} = 0.4713$$
$$a_{MH} = 0.1793$$
$$a_{LX} = 0.4134$$
$$Z = 0.4081$$
$$V_H = 0.0916$$
$$d_W = .99$$
$$d_r = .6625$$

To carry out the simulations, the following variables will be manipulated according to their actual variation:
1.   The exchange rate (e);
2.   The nominal wage rate (w);
3.   The world price of exports (P_X*).
The manipulation of P_X* has a specific purpose in the sense that I shall attempt to measure the impact of the variation of the terms of trade on aggregate demand. By holding the world price of imports (P_M*) constant and equal to unity, the fluctuation of the terms of trade over a period will be denoted by how close or how far the (manipulated) value of P_X* will depart from unity. Thus if we set $P_X* = 1$, this means that the terms of trade showed no variation during the year. A value of $P_X* < 1$ will, of course, mean that the terms of trade turned against Peru during the period and a value of $P_X* > 1$ will show just the opposite.

Period 1975-1976

During this period, the effective devaluation rate was 37 percent(12)and the nominal wage rate rose approximately 29 percent.(13)

On the other hand, the terms of trade showed a positive variation of 8.7 percent. Therefore:

$$e = 1.37$$
$$w = 1.29$$
$$P_X* = 1.087$$

The results are the following:

TABLE 10

EMPIRICAL SIMULATION FOR THE PERIOD 1975-1976: PREDICTION OF AGGREGATE VARIABLES

	1975	1 9 7 6 (predicted)	(actual)	Variation (%) (predicted)	(actual)
Home-goods Output					
$X_H = C+I+G$	681663	688852		(+) 1	(+).5
G.D.P.					
nominal	627400	827751	830400		
at constant					
market prices	627400	633321		(+) 1	(+) 2
Multiplier	2.7970	2.7370			

Note:

The predicted variation of Home-goods output and GDP at constant market prices have been obtained by subtracting the 1975 value from the predicted value of 1976 and then dividing the results by the 1975 value. The figures for the actual variation have been calculated from INE, Cuentas Nacionales del Perú 1950-1980 and from a World Bank computer run that shows Peru's main aggregate indicators based on estimates from INE.

TABLE 11

EMPIRICAL SIMULATION FOR THE PERIOD 1975-1976: PREDICTION OF INCOME SHARES (%)

	1975	1 9 7 6 (predicted)	(actual)
Labor Y_w	64	61	65
Profit Y_R	36	39	35

Note:

Actual shares of 1976 were obtained from The World Bank, Perú: Principales Cuestiones.... Cuadro II.5, p.91.

TABLE 12

EMPIRICAL SIMULATION FOR THE PERIOD 1975-1976:
PREDICTION OF PRICES

| | 1975 | 1976 | Variation (%) | |
			Predicted	Actual
P_H	1	1.3121	(+) 31.21	(+) 33.5
P_X	1	1.4892	(+) 49	(+) 46
P_M	1	1.37	(+) 37	(+) 34
Real Wage	100	98.31	(-) 1.7	(-) 0.5

Note:

Figures for the actual variation were obtained from the World Bank computer run.

A glance at the actual and predicted results reveals, in broad terms, that neither home goods output nor the gross domestic product at pre-devaluation factor prices dropped in 1976 despite an effective devaluation rate of 37 percent. The most persuasive explanation for this is that nominal wages rose 29 percent, an increase which comes close to an overall domestic price rise of 31.21 percent and which thus almost wipes out any possibility of a strong fall in aggregate demand through a drop in the real wage. Another reason is that the terms of trade were favorable. In any case, two points are relevant for this study:

1. In actual terms, despite the fact that devaluation did not bring about an absolute fall in X_H, its rate of growth for the period 1975-1976 ((+) 0.5 percent) compares unfavorably with the rate of growth in 1974-1975, which was (+)3 percent. The same point could be argued for the variation of gross domestic product at constant market prices, which increased by 4.5 percent in 1974-1975 but just 2 percent in 1975-1976.

2. The model predicts the real trend well. Even the estimate of the gross domestic product, which does not have much relevance to this study, is reasonably close.

With regard to the variation of the functional income shares, the model somewhat overestimates the profit shares. Nevertheless, it does show a trend which will be more obvious in the following years, to the degree that the economic slump takes hold. Finally, with respect to the variation of price indices, it can be seen that the model's prediction is fairly accurate.

Period 1976-1977

The major components of gross domestic product are shown in Table 9. During this period, the effective devaluation rate was 56 percent(14) and the nominal wage rate variation was 32 percent.(15)

64

The terms of trade showed a positive variation of 5.6 percent. Therefore, the new values are:

e = 1.56
w = 1.32
$P_X^* = 1.056$

The results of the simulation are as follows:

TABLE 13

EMPIRICAL SIMULATION FOR THE PERIOD 1976-1977
PREDICTION OF AGGREGATE VARIABLES

	1976	1977 (predicted)	1977 (actual)	Variarion % Predicted	Actual
X_H	879400	873292		(-) 0.7	(-)1.4
G.D.P.					
nominal	830400	1121180	1143000		
constant	830400	816011		(-) 1.7	(-)0.1
Multiplier	2.7370	2.6330			

Note:

For calculations and sources see Note in Table 10.

TABLE 14

EMPIRICAL SIMULATION FOR THE PERIOD 1976-1977
PREDICTION OF INCOME SHARES (%)

	1976	1977 (predicted)	1977 (actual)
Y_w	65	60	63
Y_R	35	40	37

Note:

For sources see Note in Table 11.

TABLE 15

EMPIRICAL SIMULATION FOR THE PERIOD 1976-1977:
PREDICTION OF PRICES

	1976	1977	Variation (%) Predicted	Actual
P_H	1	1.3862	(+)38.6	(+)38
P_X	1	1.6474	(+)64.7	(+)61
P_M	1	1.56	(+)56	(+)52
Real wage	100	95.22	(-) 4.7	(-) 4

Note:

For sources see Note in Table 12.

The results show that, in actual terms, the economy started to show clear signs of a slump. This is expressed by the fact that the multiplier has declined from 2.7370 to 2.6330. Significantly, total resources (X_H) show a real decline by -1.4 percent and gross domestic product at constant prices declined slightly. The simulation captures this trend reasonably well by predicting a -0.7 percent fall in X_H and a -1.7 percent fall in the gross domestic product.

With regard to the variation in income shares, the model gives a close prediction which, by now, is describing an actual, rapidly deteriorating income distribution against labor income. Also, with respect to the prices, the model gives close approximations.

Period 1977-1978

The major components of gross domestic product are shown in Table 9. To predict the actual figures for 1978, an increase in the nominal wage of 36 percent was considered. During this year, however, the terms of trade turned against Perú by approximately 7.88 percent. With regard to the variation of the exchange rate, the data show that in nominal terms, the Peruvian sol was devalued 90 percent in 1977. This, however, is a gross underestimate insofar as it does not adequately measure the rate of effective devaluation. In fact, Bhagwatti and Krueger(16) illustrate that the nominal changes in the exchange rate can not reveal the real magnitude of the impact of devaluation if it is accompanied by elimination (introduction) of bonuses and taxes on exports as well as on imports and if, to some extent, the exchange rate, although adjusted up, is still fixed and controlled by the government. For example, a nominal devaluation can have little or no effect if export bonuses and quantitative restrictions and surcharges on imports are removed at the same time. In the case of Peru, however, the types of exchange-rate policies adopted in

1977 led to an effective rate of devaluation higher than the nominal rate for the following reasons:

1. The authorities decided to float the sol, thus allowing the free forces of supply and demand on the foreign exchange market determine the market price of the US dollar. This mechanism insures that the market price of foreign exchange will increasingly assume a predominant role in the allocation of foreign exchange throughout the economy and not a controlled price of foreign exchange which would be given by a nominal rate of devaluation. Although the authorities decided to float in the second semester of 1977, by late that year, the exchange rate was over 140 soles per dollar. Due to the grave economic distortions produced by this policy, the government decided to freeze the rate at S/.130.

2. Export activities were greatly stimulated by the presence of the CERTEX (tax reimbursements to exporters) which were introduced in 1968, and were showing great increases by 1977. This trend was carried over to 1978. In essence, this is an export bonus which is aimed at making export ventures more profitable.

3. On the side of imports, they were greatly restricted by the introduction of a legal disposition that forced the private and public sectors to finance imports of goods and services 180 days in advance. In essence, what this implies is a type of financial tax borne by importers and thus, a higher price on them. Also, although it is impossible to make an accurate assessment, the great outlays for military spending which took place in 1977 might have made the competition for--and scarcity of--foreign reserves with the private sector more acute.

Given all these considerations, the assumed value of the exchange rate will reflect the effective rate of devaluation which is assumed to be 140 percent and not 90 percent. Therefore, the manipulated parameters take on the following values:

$$e = 2.40$$
$$w = 1.36$$
$$P = .9212$$

TABLE 16

EMPIRICAL SIMULATION FOR THE PERIOD 1977-1978:
PREDICTION OF AGGREGATE VARIABLES

| | 1977 | 1 9 7 8 | | Variation (%) | |
		(predicted)	(actual)	Predicted	Actual
X_H	1191600	1148436		(-)3.6	(-)6.3
GDP					
nominal	1143000	1825285	1854300		
constant	1143000	1121021		(-)1.9	(-)0.7
Multiplier	2.6330	2.2792			

Note:
For calculations and sources see note in Table 10.

TABLE 17

EMPIRICAL SIMULATION FOR THE PERIOD 1977-1978
PREDICTION OF INCOME SHARES (%)

	1977	1 9 7 8 (predicted)	(actual)
Y_W	63	54	60
Y_R	37	46	40

Note:

For sources see note in Table 11.

TABLE 18

EMPIRICAL SIMULATION FOR THE PERIOD 1977-1978
PREDICTION OF PRICES

	1977	1978	Variation (%) Predicted	Actual
P_H	1	1.6467	(+) 58	(+) 64.6
P_X	1	2.21	(+) 89	(+) 121
P_M	1	2.40	(+) 105	(+) 140
Real Wage	100	82.59	(-) 16.8	(-) 17.41

Note:

For sources see note in Table 12.

As can be seen, the actual trends of the economy in 1977 showed a pronounced slump. Total resources or home goods output suffered a net decrease of -6.3 percent. This trend has been portrayed by the empirical simulation which shows a drop of -3.6 percent. The actual data for gross domestic product at constant prices show a decline by -0.7 percent. The model does capture it, showing a variation of -1.9 percent.

Going over to the fluctuations of income shares, the model continues to predict the deteriorating trend against labor--which by 1979 had a share of 57 percent--although the predicted trend is somewhat overstated when compared with the official data. However, the deterioration of the real wage is predicted with remarkable accuracy. The prediction for the consumer price index is reasonably close.

In conclusion, the results derived from the empirical simulations for the three periods show conclusively that home-goods production, or total resources, contracted significantly, especially during the last period when devaluation policies were being applied strongly. The results also show that the distribution of income shifted in favor of the group of property owners. In the next section of this study I shall undertake an overall assessment of the macroeconomic effect of devaluation.

Macroeconomic Impact

The purpose of this section is to extend the analysis of the effects of devaluation for the period 1975-1978 which, as has been demonstrated conclusively in the last section, produced a negative effect on the rate of growth of the gross domestic product. At the same time, it contributed to the deterioration of an already uneven income distribution.

External Sector

To assess an overall macroeconomic impact of devaluation, I shall proceed first by evaluating the economic tendencies in the external sector. In his study "Southern Cone Stabilization Plans,"(17) Carlos Díaz Alejandro concludes that any improvement in the balance of payments has occurred, not as a result of reversing tendencies that wiped out deficits in the current account, but rather as a result of capital inflows. What can be concluded about Peru?

Let us first examine the trade balance. The deficits of 1975, 1976, and 1977 were totally erased by 1978 which showed a surplus of $48400 million, an impressive figure by all accounts, given the huge deficits which existed previously. What is important to ascertain is whether this positive fluctuation depended basically on endogenous factors such as the power of exchange-rate adjustment and the rapid reallocation of resources in favor of export and import substituting activities, or whether such a reversal in the trade balance is due more to the role of exogenous factors such as the existence of improved world prices for exports.

On the side of exports, there was an accumulated growth of 27.4 percent at constant prices from 1975 to 1978. Throughout this period, the fishing products saw their relative participation in the total value of exports decline from 16 percent to 12 percent. The agricultural products declined from 30 percent to 15 percent. On the other hand, mining products increased their share from 46 percent to 56 percent, as did the non-traditional products, from 8 percent to 17 percent. A closer look at these variations is in order:

1. The relative decline in fishing products masks the fact that during the period under consideration, there was an absolute increase in the total value exported. However, such an increase was very modest, and was due entirely to the more favorable prices for fishmeal, which more than doubled in the period 1975-1977. Not surprisingly, the volume of exports (quantum) declined, thus reflecting the serious natural constraints which confront this industry.

2. The relative decline of agricultural exports on total exports has been accompanied by an absolute decline in total value from $386.7 million in 1975 to $281.2 million in 1978. This could be explained by the erratic economic factors that affected the three main products (coffee, sugar, and cotton). In the case of sugar, its world price dropped dramatically throughout the period. This product has been recognized as the only one which is also consumed internally and therefore, is likely to be released immediately for export once demand contraction policies are introduced.(18)

In the case of coffee and cotton, both enjoyed good international prices, expecially the former; but, sharp increases in exportable volume did not take place for either of them due to bad weather conditions and limits in available capacity. In any case these events demonstrate what has been stated before. Namely, development efforts based on the export of these products require costly irrigation projects to expand capacity on the one hand, and some sort of control on world prices to prevent downward erratic fluctuations.

3. Turning now to mining products, the relative increase on total exports was accompanied by an absolute increase which almost doubled total value from $590.9 million in 1975 to $1091.9 in 1978. These products have long been recognized as representing the backbone of the structure of Peruvian exports. The main products and their relative share on total mining exports are the following:

TABLE 19

TOTAL VALUE OF MINING EXPORTS, 1975 AND 1978
(millions of dollars)

	1975	%	1978	%
Exports	590.9	100	1091.9	100
Copper	155.7	26	408.6	38
Iron	51.9	9	73.8	7
Silver	146.3	25	206.9	19
Lead	41.9	7	89.7	8
Zinc	151.5	26	133.1	12
Oil	43.6	8	179.8	16

Source: Banco Central de Reserva, Memoria 1978.

It is particularly significant to highlight the fact that, with the exception of zinc, all minerals increased total value of production in absolute terms. Nevertheless, I am interested in pointing out the two minerals which had the most significant increases, copper and oil. For the former, the increase was due to more favorable world prices, but more significantly, to the

70

increase in export volume which, by 1977, was twice that of 1975. This fact is explained by the operation of the new mine of Cuajone which began in 1976, a major investment project which took five years to mature. By the same token, the increase in oil exports can be entirely attributed to the fact that the oil pipeline was finished in 1978. Thus, the oil found in the Selva could be transported to the major export centers on the coast.

Implicit in what has been stated above is the idea that the positive developments which took place in the export sector are to be explained by the expansion of available capacity. This requires investment projects of long gestation periods and favorable international prices. The latter are determined mainly by economic conditions in the industrialized countries: at the time of this writing, the prices for copper and silver are very low in comparison with the high peaks of 1979 and 1980. Again, the country is facing serious balance of payments difficulties. On the other hand, investments aimed at enlarging supply capacity of minerals depend to a great extent on international demand and the profitability is limited by the existence of substitutes.

It is not unfair to conclude, therefore, that the significant export expansion of minerals from 1976 to 1978 was basically independent of the exchange rate policies applied during that period. Capital investment decisions on copper and oil were made at a time when it was already known that the Peruvian sol was overvalued.

4. Finally, let us consider the non-traditional exports. From 1975 to 1978, the total value of these exports increased from $107.5 million to $343.5 million and its relative share on total exports rose from 8 to 17 percent.

Before drawing any conclusions, let us first see what products are included in this category. Accordingly, the main non-traditional exports and their relative share on total exports of this sector are as follows:

TABLE 20

NON-TRADITIONAL EXPORTS, 1976 AND 1978

	1976 (%)	1978 (%)
Agricultural	11	11
Textiles	21	29
Fishing	22	15
Refined metals and Minerals (a)	24	26
Chemicals	10	9
Other (b)	12	10

(a) Includes metals, metalurgy, minerals
(b) includes paper, leather, ceramics, wood.
Source: Organización de los Estados Americanos, Informes Económicos de corto plazo, Vol. VII, 1982, Perú.

The expansion of the export market for these products has been substantial. The trend even continued until 1979, which registered an increase in total export value of 120 percent with respect to 1978 and represented 21.6 percent of total exports. By that year, this sector contributed the second most important export item, after copper.

It is likely, given the nature of these products, that devaluation has played a significant role in export growth. Apparently, therefore, there has been a positive response to devaluation policies, and this success represents the theoretical foundation for the policies that advocate a shift in the strategy of development away from import substitution and toward export promotion. The latter is regarded empirically as being superior.(19)

The appropriateness of a shift to this strategy will be considered briefly in the next chapter. At this point, however, I would like to point out two important factors that have played just as significant a role as devaluation for the promotion of non-traditional exports:

a)   The extremely low marginal costs, in this case the low cost of labor, reinforced by the significant drop in real wages.

b)   The role of CERTEX (tax reimbursements), which provided a great stimulus. In 1972, 51 percent of total non-traditional exports were under the CERTEX scheme, whereas by 1977 that percentage had risen to 75 percent.

In conclusion, therefore, devaluation did not play a positive role in the expansion of exports of traditional products. In the case of the expansion of non-traditional exports, John Sheahan argues that they did respond positively to devaluation,(20) although the dynamism of this sector was aided greatly by the low cost of wages and by tax reimbursements.

Going over to the side of imports, throughout 1975-1978 there was a negative growth rate of 40 percent for that period in real terms. There are several reasons which explain this:

1.   The peaks of 1973-1974 were abnormally high because the government, as stated before, undertook massive capital investment projects which matured in 1978.

2.   The negative level of foreign reserves.

3.   The successive devaluations.

4.   Legal dispositions to cut imports such as the requirement to deposit the import bill 180 days in advance.

Therefore, it can be seen that there were diverse types of factors playing a role in the substantial drop of imports. One positive factor was the fact that the country, by 1978, did not need to import oil or related products since the oil pipeline had gone into operation, thus permitting home consumption and even an export surplus. But, on the other hand, there were also conscious government policies aimed at reducing the import bill which, in the end, affected the purchase of vital foreign goods that were required for domestic production. In this sense, given that most Peruvian imports are price inelastic, devaluation policies pose a challenge to the local industrial firms: the fittest in all likelihood will survive (basically the oligopolistic firms), but the existing small firms vying for imported goods must necessarily feel the pinch of higher costs and consequently lower profits.

The substantial drop in imports can be illustrated by glanc-
ing at the trends for the two most important Peruvian import
items, raw materials and intermediate products and capital goods.
With respect to the former, total value of imports dropped from
$1371 million in 1975 to $771 million in 1978, whereas the latter
dropped from $958 million in 1975 to $577 million in 1978.

It is very difficult, if not impossible, to find evidence that
devaluation has stimulated recovery by reallocating production in
the direction of import substitutes. Instead, it is much more
plausible to argue that devaluation was increasingly used as a
device to ration the desperately low levels of foreign exchange.
In the end, the subsequent reduction of imports and the reversal
of the trade balance were achieved simultaneously but, as will be
shown below, at the expense of the contraction of industrial
output.

In the Peruvian case, the capacity to import is definitely
limited by the availability of foreign exchange. By 1977, the
level of foreign exchange reserves was negative, for all practical
purposes, and as such it must have had a negative effect on the
level of imports. However, under the assumption that oligopolistic
industrial firms are either tied to or enjoy credit from foreign
concerns, in theory they will eventually be able to meet foreign
bills no matter how expensive they are in soles. In my opinion,
there exists a more powerful reason that explains the fall in
imports. In essence, this is the fall in aggregate demand, in
which devaluation does play a role by inducing relative price
changes that lead to a drop in the real wage. In other words,
what I postulate is that the demand for Peruvian imports is
basically sensitive to the volumes of production of all those
final products in which imports are used as inputs. Once the
domestic demand for these final products falls as a result of
contraction, local producers, behaving according to oligopolistic
market usage, are expected to adjust their production levels and
thus indirectly lower demand for foreign inputs.

Before turning our attention to the capital account, let us
consider one of the most significant items of the current account,
that is, the flow of interest payments and dividends. In 1975,
there was a net outflow of $240 million of which $193 million
corresponded to interest on foreign debt and $47 million were
outpayments for royalties and dividends of foreign firms' investments. By 1978, these amounts were $420 million and $157 million
respectively for a total net outflow of $577 million. This
reflects the growing burden of the foreign debt and also the high
remittances abroad by foreign firms operating within the country.

Finally, with respect to the capital account the period 1975-
1978 shows the following characteristics:

1. The net inflow of long-term capital declined from $1135
million in 1975 to $421 million in 1978. This flow is broken
down as follows:

73

TABLE 21

LONG-TERM CAPITAL FLOWS, 1975 AND 1978
(millions of dollars)

	1975	1978
Private sector	342.3	38.8
investment	315.7	25.0
loans	26.6	13.8
Public	792.7	382.5
Official loans		
net	792.7	393.7
loans	1076.6	850.2
payments	283.9	456.2
Other		-11.2

Source: INE, Cuentas Nacionales del Perú 1950-1980.

As can be seen, what is of particular significance is how foreign private investment contracted, reflecting a general wariness about the economic, financial, and political situation in Peru during that period. With regard to public loans, it is important to highlight the substantial burden of the foreign debt, reflected by the fact that payments on past debts increased in 1978 by $172 million with respect to the amount reached in 1975. In essence, this is an expression of the structure of the foreign debt contracted in the early 1970s that, in the end, imposed serious strains on the balance of payments. Finally, with respect to the new loans, they were used for investment projects, for food, and for "other." This last category is supposed to account for military purchases that were significant amounts during the period: $241 million in 1976; $527 million in 1977; and $339 million in 1978.(21)

2. Turning now to short-term capital flows, there was a net outflow of $150 million in 1975; $387.7 million in 1976; $114.3 million in 1977; and $75.5 million in 1978 (see Table 5). These balances reflect nothing but the role of the expectations of the main economic agents whose fortunes are tied to developments in the external sector. Included in this are not only exporters, but also the sectors using foreign exchange for imports of consumer durables and intermediate goods, and financial institutions acting in formal and informal markets. As can be noted, the behavior of these agents reflected distrust in the overall economic and political situation.

Conclusion

By 1978, the balance of payments had improved considerably with respect to the situation in 1975, 1976, and 1977. This tendency became even more apparent in 1979. This improvement is described and explained as follows:

1.   Improvement was essentially fostered by positive develop- ments in the current account and not in the capital account.

2.   With the exception of non-traditional exports, there is very little evidence that devaluation played a significant role in the expansion of traditional exports, which basically responded to an enlarged supply capacity and favorable world prices.

3.   Reversal in the trade balance was aided greatly by a drastic cut in imports.

4.   Significant inflows of foreign capital came not from private sources but from foreign official sources. This inflow, however, was offset greatly by the ever-increasing outpayments on past foreign debt.

It is safe to conclude, therefore, that the improvement in the trade balance was more a function of exogenous factors (prices) and past investment projects (enlarged supply) than short-term economic policies (devaluation). To explain the relative slackness in the movements of the capital account (as opposed to the experience of the Southern Cone countries) involves the consideration of many diverse variables. The most important of these is the politico-economic climate, uncertain expectations, and the possible fact that the government was decided on the purchase of military equipment, much of it from the Soviet Union.

Productive Sector

In the last section, it was shown conclusively how devalua- tion had a negative effect on the growth of home-goods output and gross domestic product. Particularly, it was shown that this tendency was especially accentuated in the years 1976-1977 and 1977-1978.

It is possible to draw the same conclusion by noting that in the period 1975-1978 aggregate consumption grew by 6.8 percent in real terms and aggregate investment declined by an astonishing 56.5 percent in real terms in the same period. The slump was ag- gravated in the last two periods:

TABLE 22
RATES OF GROWTH OF CONSUMPTION AND INVESTMENT, 1975-1978
(in real terms)

YEAR	CONSUMPTION	INVESTMENT
1975	5.2	-4
1976	3.6	-12.5
1977	3.4	-26.0
1978	-5.4	-14.0

Source: Calculated from INE, Cuentas Nacionales del Perú 1950-1980.

This substantial contraction in aggregate demand would have produced a larger slump in gross domestic product were it not for the fact that there was a positive export response. But, as has been seen above, such response should be properly attributed to the play of exogenous forces.

Turning now to the specific economic sectors, it is not surprising to see that the most dynamic sectors are the ones tied to the export sector. Among these, mining stands out, as expected, with an accumulated growth rate of 29.0 percent in real terms during 1975-1978, and fishing, which had an accumulated growth rate of 20 percent.(22) Agriculture, however, which might have been expected to gain by exporting some products had a meager growth, reflecting capacity constraints and dependence on natural forces (weather).

The sectors tied to the domestic market suffered most: manufacturing and construction. The latter showed a negative growth rate of almost 19 percent in real terms for the same period.(23) This sector is particularly affected during times of demand contraction and, given its linkages and its capacity to absorb employment, it is likely to spread negative effects, especially throughout the urban areas.

It will be of major interest to consider the manufacturing sector which caters most of its production to the domestic market. As was stated before, this sector is heavily dependent on the imports of foreign inputs. Thus, its performance depends on the availability of foreign exchange, but mainly on the levels of aggregate demand which steadily contracted during the period under consideration, especially during the last two years. This can be seen more clearly by examining the indices of the volume of the manufacturing sector for the period 1975-1978 using the base year 1973 = 100.

TABLE 23

VOLUME OF PRODUCTION OF THE MANUFACTURING SECTOR, 1975-1978

	1975	1976	1977	1978
Consumer goods industry (food, drinks, textiles, shoes, tobacco, furniture, clothing, etc.)	112.1	115.2	106.5	100.8
Intermediate products (fishmeal, leather, wood, paper, chemicals, refined oil, rubber, glass, minerals, metals)	120.6	133.1	136.8	138.7
Capital Goods (machinery, electric goods, etc.)	129.1	126.8	112.2	93.2

Source: Organización de los Estados Americanos, Informes Económicos de Corto Plazo, Vol. VII , 1981, Perú, p.60.

pronounced slump can be observed in the supply of consumer
capital goods, with the decline more dramatic in the latter.
This evidence is very serious especially when considering
Schydlowsky's contention that this sector had idle capacity.
With respect to intermediate goods, however, the evidence of a
slump is far from conclusive, showing instead a slight increase
from 1976 to 1978. The answer to this is revealed by the fact
that this subsector is made up, to a large degree, by products
which have an outlet as non-traditional exports, such as wood,
chemicals, refined oil, refined minerals and metals. Thus, their
fortunes are not strictly tied to the conditions of the domestic
market.

Fiscal and Monetary Policy

Thorp, Boloña, and Herzka cite the impossibility of reversing
the overall fiscal deficit which by 1977 was still 9.4 percent of
the gross domestic product for the following reasons:(24)
1.   The government was unwilling to lower drastically current
expenditures because military spending remained an overriding
priority and also because public employees resisted substantial
cuts in their real wages.
2.   When the recession set in, it affected current revenues
because of lower margins and tax evasion.
3.   Whatever improvement may have come in the state enterprises was the result of higher prices which fueled a higher cost
of living. This, in turn, prompted further increases in the wages
of the employees of the public sector.
4.   The most effective real cuts, therefore, were in the
area of capital investment. This was reflected in the reduction
of imports by the state.
Devaluation also played a role in the general inability to
reduce current state expenditure, by elevating the relative share
of total central government expenditures going to pay interest
and principal on the foreign debt. In 1975, the payments of
interests constituted 7.2 percent of state expenditures of which
roughly 50 percent were on the foreign debt. By 1978 that share
had risen to 16.5 percent of which 53 percent corresponded to
foreign debt. On the other hand, the repayments on principal
were, in 1975, 9.8 percent of total state expenditures, of which
46 percent were on foreign debt; by 1978, the share was 17.7
percent of which 80 percent was directed toward the foreign debt.
With respect to monetary policy, contraction came primarily
in the form of credit restraint. Despite the fact that the total
money supply grew in absolute terms by 48.5 percent in 1975-1976,
by 24 percent in 1976-1977, and by 51 percent in 1977-1978, real
liquidity, in other words, the domestic monetary base adjusted
for the variation in the price level, actually dropped by 19.6
percent in 1975-1976, 2.1 percent in 1976-1977, and 6.4 percent
in 1977-1978. Thorp, Boloña, and Herzka argue that, given the
rigidity in state expenditures, the drop in real liquidity was
felt mostly in the private sector. This consequently created a
credit squeeze that must have sent many private sector firms to
the informal financial market.

Income Distribution

In the last section, it was proven conclusively that income distribution deteriorated as a result of devaluation during 1975-1978.

Before attempting to identify which sectors benefited the most and which suffered, let us first state that devaluation has been a prime factor for the historically abnormally high rate of inflation that occurred during the period, and which has been adequately explained by the model. Thus, inflation basically has got to be recognized as cost-push, given the slack capacity and all the policies applied to contract demand. The mechanism of this inflation has been the higher input costs brought about by devaluation which were passed on to the consumers.

In the last section it was seen how the real wage contracted significantly. The result was that workers were worse off after the devaluation and the related stabilization policies. On the side of the property owners, all firms caught in the credit squeeze must have seen their profitability margins sharply reduced if they were finally forced to go to the informal financial markets where the "loan sharks" rule. To the extent that these firms are able to pass on higher interest costs, this must have fueled inflation as well.

The informal sector also must have suffered to the extent that it derives part of its dynamism from the activities of the formal manufacturing sector. As has been shown, this sector significantly reduced its volume of output given the demand contraction.

At the same time, it is clear that exporters have benefited greatly during the crisis. With regard to exporters of tradi-tional products, foreign firms must have benefited from high revenues, and the state should have accumulated some of this through income taxation. This is applicable in the case of copper but not in the case of oil. An agreement signed with the foreign firms in the early 1970s provided for the split of the crude and no taxation of the profits. On the other hand, the exporters of non-traditional products are likely to have reaped windfall profits favored by the continued devaluation, by the drop in the real wage, and by CERTEX.

With respect to the large oligopolistic industrial firms, which structurally are the backbone of the domestic manufacturing sector, it is difficult to make an a priori assessment as to whether they benefited or lost during the crisis. Surely they must have been affected by the demand contraction though they could ride this out by lowering production; normal profitability margins must have been supported by the drop in wages, and, although the model assured a constant mark-up, it is possible as well that it could have been raised to maintain the profit margins. Due to their size and foreign ties, it is unlikely that there have been undue financial strains on these firms.

Finally, benefits have also been derived from speculative and financial activities. In the former one has to consider the hectic purchase of foreign inputs which were later stocked and which was done reflecting the certainty of devaluation measures.

On the other hand, banks and other financial institutions operating in the formal markets must have benefitted when the rate of interest was liberalized in the period 1977-1978. The real drop in liquidity which took place throughout the entire period of stabilization must have benefitted financial firms operating in the informal financial sector by charging high interest rates to small industrial firms caught in the credit squeeze.

NOTES

[1]Michael Kalecki, Selected Essays in the Dynamics of the Capitalist Economy, 1930-1970 (Cambridge, England: Cambridge University Press, 1971).

[2]The discussion that follows is based on the insights of Alfred S. Eichner and J. A. Kregel, "An Essay on Post-Keynesian Theory: A new Paradigm in Economics", Journal of Economic Literature, 8 (1975), 1293-1314.

[3]Instituto Nacional de Planificación: Modelo de Simulación INP-1, 1973. Cited from Carlos Boloña, La Aplicación de un Modelo Econométrico a la Economía Peruana: Un Ejercicio Metodológico (Lima, Perú: Universidad del Pacífico, Centro de Investigación, 1976), p.120.

[4]This theoretical mechanism of devaluation has been addressed by Carlos Díaz Alejandro, "A Note on the Impact of Devaluation and the Redistributive Effect", Journal of Political Economy Vol.LXXXI (1963), 577-580, and by Richard N. Cooper, "Currency Devaluations in Developing Countries", Essays in International Finance, No.86 International Finance Section, Department of Economics, Princeton University, Princeton, N.J. (1971).

[5]Reproduced in Cline and Weintraub, op.cit., pp. 465-506.

[6]Lance Taylor, Macro Models for Developing Countries (McGrawHill, Inc., 1979), p.55.

[7]Reproduced in Cline and Weintraub, op.cit., Chapter Eleven.

[8]According to Fitzgerald, op.cit., p. 268.

[9]Miguel Bacharach, "Degree of Monopoly and Income Distribution in Three Branches of the Peruvian Manufacturing Sector 1965-1975" (unpublished Master's Dissertation, 1980).

[10]Cited in Boloña, op.cit., p.120.

[11]Cited in Boloña, op.cit., p.120.

[12]González Izquierdo, op.cit., p. 183.

[13]This rate has been calculated by measuring the yearly variation of nominal earnings of salaried workers, though excluding the same variations of independent workers. Source: The World Bank, Perú: Principales Cuestiones y Recomendaciones en materia de Desarrollo, p. 96.

80

(14)González Izquierdo, op.cit., p. 183.

(15)The World Bank, Perú: Principales Cuestiones.... op.-cit., p.96.

(16)J. Bhagwati and A. Krueger, "Exchange Control, Liberalization, and Economic Development", American Economic Review, Papers and Proceedings (May 1973), 419-427.

(17)Díaz-Alejandro, "Southern Cone Stabilization Plans", op.cit., p.8.

(18)Thorp and Whitehead, op.cit., p. 124.

(19)Bhagwati and Krueger, op.cit., 420-421. A more detailed description of their empirical findings can be found in Jagdish N. Bhagwati, Foreign Trade Regimes and Economic Development: Anatomy and Consequences of Exchange Control Regimes (New York: National Bureau of Economic Research, 1978) and Anne O Krueger, Foreign Trade Regimes and Economic Development: Liberalization Attempts and Consequences (New York: National Bureau of Economic Research, 1978).

(20)Sheahan, op.cit., p. 18.

(21)According to estimates of Banco Central de Reserva del Perú.

(22)Calculated from INE, Cuentas Nacionales del Perú 1950-1980.

(23)Ibid.

(24)Thorp, Boloña, and Herzka, op.cit.

V
Alternative Approaches

The objective of this chapter is to present an alternative theoretical view of the nature of the Peruvian economy. The importance of this effort should not be underestimated since the ideas that will be presented below represent an attempt to disclose the complexities of economic, social, institutional, and political phenomena which are unlikely to be captured by the conventional economic analysis of a market society. Therefore, by incorporating these complex phenomena into my analysis, I expect to attain a richer understanding of the nature and characteristics of the Peruvian crisis of 1975 and thus to be able to provide a better assessment of the appropriateness of stabilization policies in general and devaluation in particular. In order to accomplish this goal, this chapter will resort to the theoretical tools embodied in the concept of mode of accumulation or, which is the same thing, political economy.

Before defining more properly this concept and highlighting its usefulness as a theoretical tool, let us first point out that this concept can be approximated to the ideas of strategies of development that were used in the second chapter. This similarity resides in the fact that both concepts stress the types of economic policies that are applied in a specific model of development. For example, let us take the laissez-faire strategy or export-led model of development; in this strategy, which was put into practice in Peru until the late 1950s, the economic policy placed great emphasis on the free play of market forces as a dynamic vehicle to promote growth, and as such demanded very little intervention in the market by the government. A symptom of sound economic policy was the balancing of the budget and an austere monetary policy. Also, the foreign exchange rate had to reflect conditions of adequate returns for the export sector.

The concept of mode of accumulation, on the other hand, takes such policies essentially as an instrument of conscious political action designed to optimize the use of the country's economic resources for the benefit of a specific pattern of development. The key difference lies, however, in the fact that the mode of accumulation approach explicitly recognizes that such policies basically mean the legal disposition for the transference of economic resources to social classes who will spearhead the whole process of development, and who, through the dynamism of their investment and expenditure decisions, will spread the benefits to the rest of the population in such a way that the economic reproduction of society will be guaranteed. This economic reproduction, as will be unveiled below, is basically determined by the social relations of production.

To illustrate this, let us explicitly recognize the role of key social classes in the laissez-faire strategy that has been stated above. Jürgen Shuldt describes an economic policy dominated for the benefit of the alliance of the following classes: foreign capital, with ventures in agriculture and mining; the landed local oligarchy; and, a local mercantile class which profits from imports mainly of consumer goods.(1) The control by these classes of the production activities establishes a type of economic reproduction which, according to Samir Amin, has been strikingly different from the ones experienced by advanced market societies. Whereas in the latter, the reproduction of the system has been through the articulation of production of capital goods and production of consumer goods for the "masses", the reproduction of the system in a less-developed country, like Peru in the 1950s, has been labelled dependent, since it is characterized by the articulation of production for export and production or imports of luxury consumer goods which catered mainly to wealthy classes.(2)

The framework depicted above, not surprisingly, is also very useful in characterizing the strategy of industrialization via import substitution that was introduced in Peru in the 1960s. In this case, economic policies are devised and implemented for the benefit of the alliance of the following classes: an industrial class, which is made up of local industrialists, owners, and managers of transnational corporations; the urban middle class, consisting of white collar workers; and, finally, the unionized industrial workers. One can think of the manipulation of relative prices (among them the exchange rate) that characterized this stage of development as policy instruments to foster industrialization, which was being spearheaded by local industry and by transnational corporations. In previous chapters it has been described how the model ran into a dead end by the mid 1970s, setting off an economic crisis that called for the application of stabilization policies. From the point of view of the mode of accumulation or political economy approach however, what is important is to highlight the emergence and the role that the classes mentioned above had in the process of industrialization that took place in the last 20 years. In this way, the economic rationale of the industrialization process can be more properly assessed, and, therefore, the chances for achieving a much deeper understanding of the crisis will be enhanced.

The importance of using this concept of mode of accumulation is reinforced when one has to consider the fact that behind the stabilization policies applied in 1975-1978 are not merely economic actions aimed at correcting financial disequilibrium in the external sector, but also fundamentally reordering the orientation of economic policies to establish a new pattern of development. This point has been addressed by Thorp and Whitehead(3) and its relevance should not be overlooked since it opens an inquiry into the <u>direction</u> that the Peruvian economy, in particular, and Peruvian society, in general, are heading. I shall thoroughly explore the significance of this point below. At this stage, however, I want to underscore the importance of a critical feature: the establishment of a new pattern of development is directly related to the changing conditions occurring in the economy, in other words, with the overall ability of the leading productive sectors to reproduce the economic system of society. In general terms, such an ability resides in the capacity to generate and increase the economic surplus. Whenever this capacity is severely constrained, by internal or external factors, then an economic crisis is likely to occur; very often, the solution of the crisis requires a rearrangement of the social forces which made up the class alliance that was benefiting from the former policies. For example, as will be shown later, the solution of the crisis of 1975 greatly favored the economic position of local exporters while at the same time it significantly reduced the economic welfare of the industrial working class and also of small local industrialists. Moreover, a successful solution of the crisis requires the implementation of economic policies aimed at strengthening the economic position of the leading productive sectors. It is in this sense that devaluation should be understood since it greatly favored exporters at the expense of local industrialists who preferred an overvalued exchange rate.

The theoretical usefulness of the concept of mode of accumulation may be highlighted by contrasting it with the type of analysis set forth in all the preceding chapters of this study. As stated in the first chapter, the purpose and importance of this study lies in the expectation of contrasting the fundamental tenets of monetarism and structuralism with respect to the way both of them approached the roots of the crisis and the best way to ride it out. As such, the core of this investigation has basically consisted of analyzing in theoretical terms the logic of the monetarist ·approach, whereas its appropriateness as a policy tool has been empirically tested by using a model which is essentially structuralist. In methodological terms, such a task was rendered easy by narrowing the analysis down almost exclusively to market phenomena; in other words, by focusing on the central role that the price mechanism is likely to play in the reversal of external deficits, and also by resorting to the bare facts of aggregate indicators as an empirical demonstration of the fact that devaluation of the sol significantly reduced the growth of national output. As may be expected, this methodological approach contains advantages and disadvantages. One of the former is that such an approach has provided this study with the power of conclusive empirical evidence of the negative economic results brought about by devaluation policies. Nevertheless, this approach also presents some weaknesses, for it is devoid of sociological, institutional, and historical variables, whose consideration for analysis presupposes in essence a normative approach that may well end up enriching the understanding of the Peruvian economy.

It is important to recognize, nonetheless, that the model used in this study does incorporate institutional features apt to be found in a less developed country like Peru. This fact is precisely what makes the model so rich in theoretical content. However, it is important to point out that the consideration of those features is aimed at underscoring the type of economic structure predominant in less developed countries. In other words the incorporation of institutional features and assumptions is in essence an ingenious methodological device to provide an accurate description of the economy of Peru, but under no circumstances is such an incorporation an attempt to explain why the Peruvian economy presents characteristics which make it so strikingly different from the ones that are found in advanced market societies. It is through the use of the theoretical tools embedded in the concept of mode of accumulation that I expect to address this fundamental issue.

The purpose of this chapter, therefore, is to broaden the scope of my investigation in order to find reasonable ideas that might properly explain why the Peruvian economy presents the characteristics that are so well known to us by now. To make this task easier, this chapter will consist of two sections. In the first section, I will lay out the main theoretical concepts underpinning the political economy approach. The basic goal is to integrate the key elements of this tool, i.e., social classes and reproduction of society within a conceptual framework that might permit the disclosure of the dynamics of the Peruvian economic system. In order to do so, I shall discuss two conceptual frameworks: the first is the classic Marxian model which is built upon the concept of value; the second framework goes beyond value theory and instead is built around prices although it retains the key elements stated above. In the second section, I shall set out to evaluate formally the appropriateness of the stabilization policies by investigating not only the economic viability of the pattern of development (or model of accumulation) that they foster, but also the institutional capacity that the country should possess in order to undertake the venture.

Theoretical Framework

The models that will be exposed below have in common the unusual emphasis they place on those forces which guarantee the reproduction of society not only in economic terms but also in perpetuating the sort of institutional arrangements that in the end make that task possible. According to the concept of mode of accumulation, the dynamism of this socioeconomic reproduction rests upon the relationship that the economic agents have with the activities of producing society's wealth; this is another way of stating that of paramount importance is what is called in Marxist terms the social relations of production, which to a great extent determine the way the product is distributed and the social relations in this act of exchange.

The classic Marxian model attempts to depict the concrete operation of the Peruvian economy by unveiling the formation of values which are approximately expressed in the economic realm as prices but which in essence denote an economic process well embedded in specific social relations, that in the particular case of Peru, are predominantly capitalist. On the other hand, in another conceptual framework I shall consider two approaches that take as given the visible phenomena of a market economy, i.e., prices, as the starting point to investigate the economic and institutional reproduction of the Peruvian society. The strengths and shortcomings of both frameworks are to be unveiled below.

The Classic Marxian Model

In order to discuss properly this model, I shall first resort to the concept of mode of production.

In Politics and Ideology in Marxist Theory, Ernesto Laclau defines as a mode of production "...the logical and mutually coordinated articulation of:
a) a determinate type of ownership of the means of production;
b) a determinate form of appropriation of the economic surplus;
c) a determinate degree of development of the division of labor;
d) a determinate level of development of the productive forces."(4)

For the purposes of this discourse, special emphasis will be placed on discussing the first two elements, since the degree of development of the division of labor and the level of development of the productive forces can be readily identified with some visible facts of development or underdevelopment. For example, another way to express these elements is the level of total factor productivity that a country has. On the other hand, ownership of the means of production and the appropriation of the economic surplus, according to a mode of accumulation approach, play such a large role in any process of development that they cannot be ignored. Conventional economic development theory also recognizes this fact, especially the appropriation and generation of economic surplus. What heightens the interest of examining these elements in detail is my conviction that a more powerful insight could be gained by treating them with variables that lie outside the realm of pure market (economic) phenomena. The approach that follows below expects to attain this goal.

Following Laclau it is possible to state that an economic system is largely determined by a specific mode of production. In Peru, I postulate that the capitalist mode of production is predominant in the determination of the entire fabric of its socioeconomic system although there exist considerable formations which could be associated with a pre-capitalist or feudal mode of production. In this methodology, the concept of mode of production could be approximated to the concept of dualism which was used to characterize the nature of the Peruvian economy in the second chapter. As such, the pre-capitalist mode of production could be associated with the traditional sector and the capitalist mode of production could be related to the characteristics of the modern sector. It has been postulated that in Peru the latter is predominant, so I shall analyze it briefly but in some detail.

At the center of the stage is the recognition that society has a class structure which is determined by the access to and ownership of the means of production. As such, there is a capitalist class which owns and control the means of production and there are workers who historically have been dispossessed of them. Marx saw the emergence of these classes as the unfolding of a long historical process which culminated in revolutionary changes in the forces of production in Europe that brought on the disappearance of subsistence economies (where production is for use) and the emergence of industrial societies (where production is geared to the market, for exchange). This new society is characterized by an "immense accumulation of commodities"(5) which are the depository of a use-value and an exchange-value (price). The emergence of this society is ultimately determined by the presence of free wage laborers who have been divested of their own means of production.

In order to disclose the foundation on which the entire fabric of capitalist society rested, Marx devised his Labor Theory of Value. His fundamental goal was to unearth the existence of exploitation or appropriation of the economic surplus by a social class not directly related to the produce of society. As such, he went on to formulate his essential assumption of how a commodity producing society created a surplus or profit not appropriated by the direct producers (workers). Thus, in order to explain the prices of goods (commodities) in the market, Marx had to trace them back to the real production process which gave rise to them.

In order to find an answer to this problem it is imperative to take a clear look at the nature of the commodity, which so dramatically characterizes the nature of a capitalist society. It was indicated above that a commodity is a depository of a use-value, in other words a characteristic that is directly related to the utility functions of the consumers and an exchange-value, which can be approximated to price. In the Marxist model, it is the exchange value of the commodity which is critical to explaining the dynamics of the whole system. As such, all analysis hereafter will be geared to this feature, which from now on will just be called value.

A commodity, therefore, has a value, which is created in the production process and which is determined by the socially necessary labor time to produce it. In order to be produced, a commodity requires the convergence, in general terms, of two factors of production: constant capital which is made up of machinery and raw materials and variable capital, which is constituted by the expense in the laborers which operate the constant capital. It should be stressed that the elements of constant capital are also commodities which have a value determined by the socially necessary labor time required to produce them.

The total value of a commodity will be composed of three parts: (a) the transferred value (to the commodity produced) of the constant capital expended in her production; (b) the expense in variable capital; (c) surplus value.

In a capitalist society creation of new values (economic growth) is made possible only by the last two components since the value of constant capital is merely a transference of value that has been created before. Of critical importance, therefore, is to analyze in detail the nature of variable capital and surplus value. In fact it is the latter, which in the act of commodity exchange appears as profit, that constitutes the key variable of the whole system. How is it created?

The answer to this puzzle lies in the twofold character of labor, namely its use-value and exchange-value. Marx calls the former labor in general, in other words, the ability labor has to produce a mass of use-values, while the latter is directly related to his fundamental concept of labor-power. As such, in order to engage in the production process and thus survive, the laborer sells the capitalist his capacity to work; the difference between the total labor time expended in production and what is needed to produce his own means of subsistence (value of labor-power) constitutes the surplus value which is appropriated by the owner of the means of production. In Marxian terms, the ratio between the surplus value and the value of labor power is called the rate of surplus value or exploitation rate. This, in essence, is the source of the economic surplus, which in Marxian terms means exploitation.

In this analysis, labor-power itself is also a commodity which the capitalist can buy to undertake production. This fact is the basic sociological insight of Marxism: that all of this market economic system--which presents an array of things and concepts that are directly observable, i.e., division of labor, competition, freedom of exchange, money, "unseen hand", etc.-- necessitates the existence of a social class that has been deprived of their own means of production and which is doomed to selling its capacity to work, i.e., labor-power, in order to survive. Therefore, this historical unfolding of the capitalist mode of production brings into a contradictory unity the capitalists and the workers, and it is Marx's theory of value which uncovers their social relations in the production process. This contradictory unity is expressed in the fact that capitalists and workers have opposing goals: the former, as owners of the means of production are interested in expanding their capital, whereas the workers, as owners of another commodity--labor power, sole creator of values--are engaged in the act of production basically to satisfy the need for survival.

On the other hand, under this framework, all distribution phenomena have to be linked with their basic foundation: production. In Marxist theory, all value added by productive labor is to take place in the production process at a given exploitation rate which itself varies according to the very dynamism of capitalist production and is basically determined by the relative strength of capitalists and workers engaged in class struggle. In this way, it is possible to question the validity of income categories, i.e., wage, profit, etc. which appear in the market as independent things, and instead assert that all those things are actually the manifestation of social relations between people.

In order to establish the applicability of this theoretical framework to the real nature of the Peruvian crisis, it is necessary to explore the inner dynamics of the capitalist mode of production, in other words, what Marx called the "laws of motion". This leads to the consideration of the key concept of accumulation. As stated above, the capitalist mode of production is characterized by the production of commodities, i.e., goods for exchange. This is the same as stating that in the capitalist mode of production value is self-expanding. What this basically means is that this mode of production emerges as the resolution of contradictory forces, namely, the use-value and the exchange-value embedded in commodities. In fact, as should be clearer shortly, the very dynamism of the system lies in the contradictory nature of the commodity: in order to survive as a viable mode of production, capitalism has to expand the production of use-values, attainable by the decrease of the exchange values.

The points stated above imply the consideration of two factors: what determines the expansion of production, and what is the mechanism to achieve it. The answer to the first issue lies in the coercive force of competition. Firms which do not grow are bound to perish. It follows, therefore, that for those firms which do not steadily seek to increase their wealth, bankruptcy will be inevitable. Hence the need to grow (accumulate). Firms which fail to meet the market standards are swept away.

This last point leads to the consideration of the second factor, namely, the mechanism of accumulation. The battle of competition among firms is fought by cheapening the commodities. Despite the fact that this phenomenon is "visible", in other words, that it takes place in the market or the sphere of exchange, it nevertheless has direct roots to the production process. This is so because the only way to cheapen commodities is by expanding production, i.e., by increasing the production of the mass of use-values. To carry this out, firms must constantly introduce changes in their production techniques, for the best way to cheapen the commodities is by having larger productive units. This will be reflected in the raising of the productivity of labor.

The success of this process depends ultimately on the ability to extract surplus value as additional exchange-value. This can be achieved absolutely, i.e., by lengthening the time of the working day. However, the most effective way to do it is relatively, i.e., by decreasing the value of labor-power, in other words, by shortening the amount of necessary labor time needed for the reproduction of the commodity labor-power or, by cheapening the goods that workers consume (their means of subsistence) which is the same thing. And, the best way to achieve this is by the introduction of changes in the production techniques.

Therefore, the inner drive to accumulate is manifested ultimately in revolutionary changes in the forces of production. However, this process of accumulation carries with itself the

seeds of an economic crisis. Marx called this the tendency of
the rate of profit to fall and is given by the fact that the
introduction of changes in production techniques implies a
gradual fall in the rate of profit (which is the "market" manifestation of the rate of surplus value that has been generated in
production) because the only element which produces surplus value
i.e., labor-power (variable capital), has decreased relatively to
the rise of constant capital (as denoted by the introduction of
new production techniques). In other words, what has taken place
is the relative expulsion of living labor from the production
process and, consequently, a scarce surplus value relative to
capital advanced. Eventually, therefore, the whole process leads
to a situation in which the "reduced labor-power is no longer
able to reproduce and enlarge the total capital, i.e., when the
expansion of production outruns its profitability".(6) This is
the situation of an economic crisis which, according to Marx,
takes the form of "overproduction, speculation, and surplus-
capital alongside surplus population".(7) In other words, the
greater mass of surplus value cannot offset the higher rise in
constant capital. Thus, the crisis, according to Mattick, is the
manifestation of the conflict between the expansion of production
and the expansion of surplus value, a conflict which has its
roots in the opposing movements of the use-value and exchange-
value of commodities. The consequence of all this is the
interruption of the accumulation process, the overproduction of
commodities and the overproduction of means of production.

The process just described reflects, in general terms, the
inner logic of a capitalist mode of production which, for Marx,
found a real expression in the situation that advanced market
societies were experiencing in the last century. How applicable
this model is to the reality of the Peruvian society will be
discussed below. Before doing so, however, it is imperative to
grasp the key ideas of the process above described. As such, it
is important to recall that the objective of the capitalist mode
of production is the reproduction of the entire economic system.
This reproduction is ensured by the process of accumulation of
capital which itself depends on the ability to extract or appropriate more surplus value. The latter, in turn, is carried out
by the expansion of commodity production, which is effectively
done by the introduction of changes in the production techniques
that aim at the shortening of the labor time embodied in a commodity. The crucial feature of this process is that the changes
in production techniques should be aimed at shortening the necessary labor time of all those commodities that are consumed by the
workers (mass consumption goods). In this way, the value of
labor power will be reduced, therefore the workers will devote
less time to produce their own means of subsistence and more time
thus will be allotted to produce the surplus value which is
appropriated by the capitalist class.

At this stage, this exposition is directed towards attempting
to apply this framework to the Peruvian crisis. Such an effort
has been carried out by John Weeks.(8) He grounds the roots of
the Peruvian crisis in phenomena taking place exclusively in the

production process and thus he dismisses Thorp's thesis that the crisis could be traced to an "unresolved constraint in export supply" given the fact that she ascribes export proceeds as the basis for capital accumulation; for Weeks, however, such an argument is not valid since it is grounded in phenomena that take place in the market sphere and not in the real production process.

Weeks describes the process of industrialization via import substitution that took place in the 1960s as the penetration of the capitalist mode of production in the Peruvian economic system, in particular, and society, in general. Given the specific characteristics of the Peruvian economy, where backwardness or pre-capitalist modes of production still exist, the economic crisis could be explained by the fact that capital accumulation has a limit to its expansion that is given by the inability of the economy to shorten the labor time in the production of workers' consumer goods (their means of subsistence). This is so because such goods are produced precisely under pre-capitalist relations of production, characterized by the relevance of outdated techniques. Therefore, the penetration and development of the capitalist mode of production is impaired by the inability to increase higher surplus value and thus continue the dynamic process of accumulation. In principle, Weeks maintains, this problem could be overcome if Peru decides to import these mass consumer goods, but this decision would increase the demand for an already scarce amount of foreign exchange that is mainly put to use for the purchase of capital goods.

This view of the crisis is indeed penetrating. In the end, Weeks argues, the economic crisis is solved by a drastic reduction of the value of labor-power, either by dismissing workers, thus increasing the unemployment rate, or by raising the prices of the industrial products relative to any increase in the money wage. The latter implies a situation in which commodities are sold at prices "above values" and this is possible where an oligopolistic market structure of industry exists. In any case, the effect will be to extract more surplus value, and thus restore the process of accumulation.

Nevertheless, the crisis will be more profound if the market position of oligopolistic industrial firms is threatened. In this case, the ability to increase surplus value by selling "above values" will be greatly diminished by the coercive force of competition. In fact, Weeks points to the penetration of the Peruvian economy by transnational corporations as evidence that this phenomena occurred in the crisis of 1975. Under these circumstances, extraction of additional surplus value will be achieved only by the dismissal of workers, as an attempt to drive down the value of labor-power. This, in turn, constitutes the basis for potential social unrest that may threaten the stability of the economic system.

Given these circumstances, therefore, the prevalence of backwardness in the productive sectors that deliver the mass consumption goods constitutes a real threat to the stability and survival of the capitalist mode of production. In principle, the inability of the capitalist mode of production to penetrate these areas could be explained by the political and economic hegemony of the landed oligarchy which was never interested in the expansion of the domestic market since the basis of their economic power resided in export activities. In Peru, however, the military regime undertook an agrarian reform that ended up eliminating the power of that class. The continuing failure to root out backwardness, therefore, has to be explained by reasons other than the political hegemony of the landed oligarchy. An alternative explanation of this fact is provided by Alain de Janvry and will be shown below.

I do not want to finish the discussion of this Marxian model without pointing out two main limitations that this approach presents:

1. A very important critique has been launched by Teobaldo Pinzás García.(9) He argues that Weeks' basic point that the workers' consumer goods are produced under pre-capitalist social relations cannot pass the test of empirical verification. Drawing from empirical studies carried out by the Instituto Nacional de Estadística about price indices of consumer goods, Pinzás concludes that about 56.1 percent of total consumption expenditures of lower income people in Lima consisted of purchases that could be considered necessities of life or means of subsistence (food and drink). Of this total, he considers that only 14.8 percent could be considered as purchases of goods produced under precapitalist relations.(10)

2. The second problem I would like to point out is methodological. It is the basic characteristic of the Marxist methodology to abstract from phenomena in the market (the "visible" facts) in order to discover the essence of things which lies hidden beneath their surface. A scientific venture has to penetrate this world of appearances, i.e., prices, wages, profits, technical change, etc., and thus bring to the open the essential features of the development of these appearances. In Marxist methodology, the best way to undertake this venture is by grasping the law of value which is firmly rooted in the social relations of production.

The theoretical framework developed above and Weeks' rigorous use of it to explain the causes of the crisis are firmly rooted in the conviction that the capitalist mode of production possesses an inner mechanism which propels the economic system to situations that are experienced in the market, i.e., inflation, recession, overproduction, etc. The law of value would be an instrument to understand this process. However, we have yet to come up with a precise and concrete definition of value. It was said above that it is an approximation of prices. However, Joan Robinson has stated that " [value] is not simple a price; it is something which will explain how prices come to be what they are. [It turns out to be], like all metaphysical concepts, just a word."(11) In other words, she goes on to imply that if the concept of value has utility at all, it is for ideology only. This in fact is a devastating attack since it questions the scientific validity of Marxist methodology. It is thus no surprise that she argues that, specifically in Marxian theory, the concept and theory of value are not necessary at all, for analysis of a Marxian type can be conducted without it. Why bother about such methaphysical concepts, such as value and surplus value, when our direct experience tells us that we deal in fact with prices, profit?

This methodological problem, as might be expected, has set off a controversial debate.(12) To deal with it, however, is beyond the scope of this study. Of particular relevance for the purpose of this investigation is that strict adherence to value theory renders the task of empirical verification (of the Marxist framework) virtually impossible. Such a staunch defender of the value theory as Fine implicitly admits this fact by stating that values exist although they can neither be observed nor even measured.(13) These issues, as it stands, escape the realm of pure logic and plunge us instead into problems of a philosophical nature.

Beyond Value Theory

In this section I shall present two alternative conceptual frameworks that also attempt to provide an understanding of the Peruvian economy in accordance to the theoretical tools of the concept of the mode of accumulation. As opposed to the classic model above depicted, these approaches take prices as given and thus assume away the existence of values.

Alain de Janvry's Framework

Implicit in the classic Marxist explanation of the Peruvian crisis (as denoted by Weeks above) is the idea that in Peru there coexist, side by side, two modes of production, one modern or capitalist and the other backward or pre-capitalist. In the former, market social relations rule whereas in the latter the economic activities are mainly for subsistence. Both modes of production are basically independent of each other. In this perspective, economic development is seen as the fulfilling of the historic mission of capitalism, that is, the breaking up of pre-capitalist social relations which have very low levels of productivity by the penetration of capitalist relations which produce more material wealth.

However, it might well be that both modes of production constitute, in fact, a particular unity embedded in a specific economic system that has evolved as a result of a long historical process shaped by national and international factors. In other words, the argument for dualism is not at all clear if one can depict a situation in which the capitalist mode of production has introduced market exchange relations in the pre-capitalist areas, but at the same time, in the interest of securing the reproduction of capital, perpetuates in the same areas social relations which are still pre-capitalist, for example, the absence of a free labor force or workers in the countryside. This issue has been raised by Laclau(14) though he admits that there is still much research to do in this area. Nevertheless, I consider this approach very useful in understanding the seemingly chaotic reality of modern Peru--several Perus, the disorganized and heterogeneous markets that I was speaking of in the second chapter.

An excellent aid indeed is provided by Alain de Janvry.(15) His goal is to explain the existence of rural poverty, i.e., "marginalization". As can be seen, this objective can be framed for the reality of Peru. His basic methodological premise consists in the interrelated articulation of three economic levels:

1.   The international level, which is denoted by the market exchange of raw materials and consumer goods (in the export-led model of development) and of raw materials and capital goods (in the import substitution strategy of development). De Janvry argues that this level is characterized by the presence of "unequal exchange", or what is approximately the same thing, adverse external terms of trade for less-developed countries. It is a situation that Cardozo characterizes by the fact that the higher productivity present in the production of capital goods by industrialized countries, when traded to the less developed countries, is not passed down in terms of lower prices because the power of unions and the oligopolistic market structures prevent it.(16)

2.   A sectoral level, which denotes the relationship between modern industries which cater their production towards satisfying the needs of the upper income classes and those industries which produce mass consumption goods (textiles, food, etc.). In this sector there is also unequal exchange, to be explained below.

3.   And finally, a social level, composed by the relationship between landlords and the marginals. The latter are defined by de Janvry as the "farmers who have lost control of their means of production because they cannot stand competitive pressure from the modern sector and nor can they [become free workers] because they cannot be absorbed by the modern sector".(17)

De Janvry's fundamental thesis is that the only way to sustain the industrialization process (via import substitution) in less developed countries is through the maintenance of cheap labor costs which definitely leads to the perpetuation of impoverishment of the marginal population. The reason for this lies in the fact that the local industrial firms, in order to absorb the unequal exchange from their international trade, pass the economic burden of it to labor through low wages because this is the only alternative to secure profits and thus remain competitive. This need, in turn, affects adversely the terms of trade with the industries which produce mass consumption goods (food, textiles), because the prices of these "necessities of life" must be kept low. This explains in part why the most technologically advanced industrial firms in less developed countries cater their production towards a demand profile of luxury consumer goods that can be afforded only by the upper income social classes. Now, with the terms of trade unfavorable for the production of food, this has to adversely affect socioeconomic conditions in the countryside. This is the sector where the most oppressive and socially unacceptable conditions of exploitation take place. In some cases, the marginals (poor peasants) could own a very small plot of land (minifundio) barely providing the means of subsistance for their families; very often it does not, so they go out to seek seasonal employment, which they can find in larger farms producing foodstuffs that are marketed in the urban areas. The landlords of these larger farms, as is known, face unfavorable prices for their products. They are able to partially offset this by paying very low wages to the marginals which are in large supply; the payment of low wages is also made possible by the fact that the marginals may partially cover their means of subsistence through working their plots.

The conclusions of this theoretical framework run contrary to Week's conclusions. In fact, what de Janvry sets out to demonstrate is that the resistance of backward areas to the penetration of the capitalist mode of production is in fact a condition for the very survival of the latter! In no other way, he seems to assert, can one explain the appalling contradictory unity of an economic system which encompasses simultaneously wealth, high unemployment and underemployment, and widespread poverty. This contradictory unity, de Janvry claims, is manifested in the three levels: at the international level, structural deficit in the balance of payments; at the sectoral level, stagnation in agriculture, which ultimately leads to inflation and the worsening of the deficit in the external sector; and, finally at the social level, miserable wages.(18)

Seminario and Cruz Saco's Framework

In "La Naturaleza del Ciclo Económico en el Perú", these authors attempt to disclose the dynamics of capital accumulation in modern Peru.(19) The work is inspired very much by a Kaleckian-Robinson framework and, while being grounded in market prices, it nevertheless uses key Marxist concepts, such as social classes, reproduction of capital, etc. The framework is described below.

In modern Peru, they argue, there are two well defined capitalist sectors, an internal industrial sector, which gears its production for the domestic markert, and an external sector, whose production is mainly directed for foreign consumption. The key determinant that permits the economic reproduction of these capitalist sectors is that both be able to obtain an adequate return on its operations, in other words, a rate of profit which permits the coverage of production costs plus an economic benefit.

In broad terms, profits will depend mostly on the rate of capital investment, which by enlarging total capital permits the raising of total productivity; also, profits will depend on the existence of an effective aggregate demand which guarantees the plowback of investment to the firms. However, it is of more relevance to denote specifically what determines profits in both sectors.

In Peru, given the structure of its exports, one can safely assume that the growth of the export sector in the long run is exogenously determined, by the demand from industrialized countries of traditional products. This exogenous demand constitutes the main incentive for investment in this sector. The capitalists expect to secure profit, which, given certain international prices and a given exchange rate, will depend on the level of nominal wages and on the level of productivity. Rising nominal wages are generally not seen as advantageous by capitalists in this sector since they lead to an increase in the price level and probably set off inflationary expectations that might cause a deterioration in the competitive position in the international markets. In principle, higher wages could be accomodated without impairing export profits if the growth of labor productivity is higher, but as the authors argue, wages are unlikely to rise given the existence of a vast supply of cheap, unskilled workers.

Turning to the internal industrial sector, its growth is greatly influenced by conditions in the external sector. In fact, economic activities in the export sector are a source of demand for capital goods and consumer goods that could be produced locally; also the proceeds of the export activities constitute the supply of foreign exchange which is badly needed by the local industrial capitalists to purchase vital foreign inputs. In the end, profits in this sector will be determined by economic conditions of domestic demand; investment decisions by capitalists will be greatly influenced by their expectations of future sales. For this sector, rising nominal wages are not a curse since they could lead to an expanded aggregate demand, especially if the productive units are operating at less than full capacity. In situations of full utilization of capacity, however, the only way that rising wages could be accomodated without lowering profits is by raising prices. This however, could set off an inflationary spiral.

Following these authors, there exists a fundamental variable which greatly influences the rate of profit and, thus, the process of accumulation of both capitalist sectors: the exchange rate. Accordingly, the authors postulate the existence of an "equilibrium" exchange rate, i.e., a price of foreign exchange that should permit the economic reproduction of both sectors considering that this price be set in accordance with equilibrium conditions in the balance of payments. For the capitalists in the export sector, the exchange rate should be set low enough to permit the generation of export proceeds which will be used and converted into soles to pay production costs and secure a profit. If there exists an overvalued exchange rate, profits in the export sector are likely to be less and will discourage investment in this sector; this, however, could be offset if there is technical change that raises labor productivity and also if exporters find high international market prices for their products. On the other hand, if exports enjoy high international prices as the exchange rate is neither overvalued nor undervalued, then they are likely to secure extraordinary profits which could prompt, the exchange rate to be revalued. This seldom happens, however, because of the instability and unpredictability of international prices. For the capitalists in the internal sector, the "equilibrium" price of foreign exchange should permit a steady industrial production at a level that satisfies the internal demand, securing an expected rate of profit. An over-valued exchange rate would foster industrialization, since it means that the cost of foreign inputs in soles would be lowered, whereas an undervalued exchange rate should discourage industria-lization because of prohibitive costs in local currency of foreign inputs.

Seminario and Cruz point out that the possibility of an exchange rate in equilibrium both for the external and internal sector is very unlikely for a country like Peru.(20) What in reality usually happens is the existence of an exchange rate above or below equilibrium for the industrial sector; the former prevails in the industrialization via import substitution strategy, and acts as an stimulus for the imports of foreign inputs. Given an initial push on demand from incomes generated in the export sector, the industrial capitalist will expand produc-tion, stimulated by an overvalued exchange rate. This, plus the likelihood of inflationary expectations, ends up discouraging accumulation in the export sector and thus the supply of foreign exchange diminishes.

So far, it should be noted, this exposition bears strong resemblance to the structuralist conceptual frameworks that have been mentioned in preceding chapters. After all, Taylor's model at the outset recognizes the existence of these separate sectors and Schydlowsky and Wicht have characterized the crisis as a situation in which the demand for foreign exchange clearly out-stripped the supply of it. However, what makes Seminario and Cruz Saco's work so much richer and particularly penetrating is the fact that they are able to identify clearly the specific class interest of both capitalist sectors and thus unveil the economic rationale of the economic policies they espouse for the state to undertake. For example, capitalists in the external sector, who in general are unconcerned with the domestic market, view with deep distrust any government intervention aimed at supporting aggregate demand, especially if such economic activity is financed through taxation that affects exporter's incomes. On the other hand, an unbalanced budget is deemed to be undesirable since it could generate inflationary pressures that might in the end deteriorate the competitive position of their exports. Finally, since their main concern is the international market, exporters in general advocate free trade because they fear foreign retaliatory policies against domestic protectionist measures. However, industrial capitalists (as distinct from export capitalists) will generally favor the enaction of commercial tariffs that will protect their products from foreign competition, and fiscal policies aimed at enlarging the demand in the domestic market.

What are, therefore, the roots of the crisis in this frame-work? For Seminario and Cruz Saco, they lie in the cyclical nature of the accumulation process in both capitalist sectors. They argue that in Peru, this accumulation process has definite limits for its further expansion that threatens the reproduction of the economic system.(21) They describe the cycle as originating essentially in the expansive phase of the economic cycle that is spearheaded by the accumulation process in the external sector. The economic activities in this sector cause a higher consumption demand in the internal market, thus creating a multiplicative effect. The industrial capitalist sector seizes this opportunity for expansion, demanding more labor and increasing the purchases of local and foreign inputs. This economic expansion in turn sets off an increase in the price level (if there exists utilization at full productive capacity or if inflationary expectations have set in) which results in the deterioration of the competitive position of the export sector, thus negatively affecting their profits. This fact, and the existence of an overvalued exchange rate (to foster industrialization) discourages the expansion in the export sector. Eventually, a crisis in the balance of payments sets in, due to the fiscal policies that supported aggregate demand (thus stimulating inflation), and to the demand pressures on foreign exchange by the industrial firms. Recovery, thus, comes about by reestablishing the profitability in the external sector, so that an adequate supply of foreign exchange can be secured. This is done by eliminating all the obstacles that hamper export profits: control of wages, devaluation, and fiscal and credit restraint. These policies naturally reduce aggregate demand and thus, affect further accumulation by the capitalists in the industrial sector. Recovery, thus, is brought about through recession. It is in this sense that the objective of devaluation should be properly understood.(22) Once the export sector has recovered, however, the pressures to satisfy internal demand set in again and the cycle is resumed.

As a final point, I would like to briefly address a very important issue. This is the consideration of how de Janvry's and Seminario and Cruz Saco's conceptual frameworks have modified the classic Marxian model described above.

As has been stated before, the main difference resides in the fact that these two approaches are based on the "visible" economic phenomena, i.e., prices. Given this fact, value theory is totally disposed of. This represents a very important modification that according to advocates of the classic model ends up obscuring the fundamental nature of the capitalist mode of production, i.e., class struggle. For example, following Seminario and Cruz Saco's framework, the process of accumulation is directly linked to the ability of capitalist firms to secure a profit. This profit, in turn, is the result of a production process in which the technical proportion of the inputs is assumed as given. In other words, profits are located in the sphere of production but they are explained as a technical matter. On the other hand, for the classic model, it is impossible to understand the nature of profits without analyzing the specific social relations of production which made them possible. The fundamental characteristic of these social relations is essentially the contradictory unity of capitalists and workers who are engaged in class struggle in the act of production. The relative bargaining position of these classes will determine a given exploitation rate or rate of surplus value which in turn will constitute the source of profits that will be appropriated by firms in the act of exchange. All this process can be adequately explained only by value analysis.

On the other hand, de Janvry's and Seminario and Cruz Saco's frameworks enrich the classic model as well. Both provide valuable insights that are likely to be put to empirical testing. De Janvry's framework is an interesting attempt to incorporate for analysis the rural backward areas which the classic model sees as antagonistic to the expansion of the capitalist mode of production. More significantly, however, is the contribution made by the pathbreaking work of Seminario and Cruz Saco. In this work, the complexity of the class structure of Peru is eased by postulating the existence of two different capitalist classes whose economic goals determine so dramatically the economic cycle. In no way does their work modify the classic model in this respect, since the differing economic goals of both capitalist classes does not preclude the existence of competition among them for the extraction of increased surplus value. Nevertheless, the rigorous analysis they offer to explain the dynamics of both capitalist sectors provides, in my opinion, valuable insight into understanding more properly the cyclical nature of the process of capital accumulation.

With this final discussion, I draw to a close the theoretical analysis of the mode of accumulation approach. As can be seen, it is of a very complex nature, but it definitely broadens the scope of the investigation by providing very rich ideas about the nature of the Peruvian economy, in general, and its crisis, in particular. In the next section, I shall make use of this theoretical framework to assess the appropriateness of the stabilization policies.

A General Evaluation

It is worth pointing out again one of the salient points mentioned above. This is the implicit recognition that stabilization policies in general, and devaluation, in particular, are applied to shift the overall orientation of the economic policies, away from measures aimed at fostering accumulation in the internal industrial sector and towards stimulating profitability in the export sector. In other words, capitalists in the export sector become the leading class and their dynamic expansion is supposed to initiate the expansive phase of the economic cycle again, increasing aggregate demand and thus stimulating production in the internal sector.

Export recovery, however, depends greatly on exogenous factors. The key point, in my opinion, is to closely evaluate the nature of export behavior or response in order to predict as reasonably as possible how quickly the balance of payments will

be able to reverse the negative trends.The importance of this process resides in its twofold nature:
1. How long are the contractionary policies necessary to sustain export recovery?
2. Do domestic and international conditions justify the need for the introduction of a new mode of accumulation (strategy of development)? In this particular case, how rational, from a political economy approach, is it to move away from import substitution industrialization to export promotion?

Let us elaborate on these points in some detail. It should be remembered, for example, how overall economic recovery set in Peru after the two crises that preceded the collapse in 1975. As was pointed out in the second chapter, the increase of the international prices of traditional exports greatly reversed the deficit in the balance of payments and fostered expansion in 1958; in the crisis of 1967, it was mentioned that the government resorted to strict austerity measures which helped weather the crisis by 1970. Both crises, however, present different political economy dimensions: by 1958, as was stated previously, the country was under an export-led mode of accumulation (laissez-faire strategy); when the crisis was over by 1959-1960, the government was still applying orthodox, free market economic measures, which, as should be clear by now, favored the interests of the landed oligarchy and mining exporters. By 1963, however, the country had decided to shift its strategy of development towards import substitution industrialization, and it did so despite the fact that from a "pure" economic point of view the orthodox policies had proved to be sound, as is evidenced by the fact that the budget and the balance of payments were in equi-librium and the inflation rate was low. The shift to another mode of accumulation, therefore, has to be explained by other factors, the most important being, in my opinion, the increasing pressure from new social groups(23) (among them an emerging urban middle class) to gain economic and political participation. This process, not surprisingly, culminated in the election of the first populist government in 1963. On the other hand, the resolution of the crisis of 1967 was characterized not by a shift to another mode of accumulation but rather by intensifying the existing one (industrialization via import substitution). In fact, a careful review of the rationale of the economic policies and reforms carried out by the military government proves that assertion reasonable; why this happened can be answered by several variables. Institutionally, for example, one can cite the emergence of a new political elite (the military) who undertook the task of enacting long overdue reforms to stave off the threat of Marxist penetration. Weeks, on the other hand, asserts that the military government was the political expression of a nascent class alliance that came to dominate the economic sphere, one composed of local industrialists and transnational corpora-tions.(24)

The crisis of 1975 deserves very special attention. The results obtained in chapter four leads to conclude that contrac-tionary policies were largely unnecesary since exogenous factors fostered export recovery. On the other hand, given the type and intensity of the deflationary policies applied, it is not entirely unreasonable to postulate that the crisis could have unleashed political and economic forces that demanded the establishment of another mode of accumulation, in this case, one based on an export promotion (of non-traditional exports) strategy. To support this argument one must remember the degree of change of the devaluation rate, how the real wage dropped substantially, the restrictive monetary policy, etc. More significant is the role of the CERTEX which stimulated the exports of non-traditional products, as was stated in the last chapter; moreover, and equally important, is the fact that this shift would be in accordance with the trend existing in the international economy, as is evidenced by the experiences of Chile (1974), Uruguay (1975), Argentina (1976).

If, as seems to be the case, the goal of the stabilization policies was to lay the ground work for the establishment of the export promotion strategy, then the relevant issue is to explore the political and economic viability of this mode of accumulation for Peru. In other words, this leads to an exploration of Thorp and Whitehead's vital concern about the direction in which the Peruvian society is heading. In order to take on this issue, I shall deal with the economic rationale of this strategy as well as its applicability to the institutional setting of Peru.

In strict economic terms, export promotion has been regarded as superior to the import substitution strategy.(25) Meier also arrives at the same conclusion, citing as reasons that export promotion saves more foreign exchange than import substitution; that the constraint of a limited home market is removed because export promotion is strictly concerned with international markets; that it could have more linkages to agriculture if "it involves the processing of primary products"(26); that it is more labor intensive; and, finally, that it could improve the existing distribution of income.

The virtues of this strategy have been further dramatized by an empirical study undertaken by Bela Balassa.(27) From a sample of ten countries which embraced this strategy in the 1960s and 1970s i.e., Korea, Taiwan, etc., and others which did not or arrived relatively late (i.e., Chile, India, Mexico), Balassa has found that "increases in per capita incomes in Korea would have been 43 percent smaller and in Taiwan 33 percent smaller, if export growth rate in these countries had been identical to the average for the sample as a whole. Conversely, increases in per capita incomes in Chile, India, and Mexico, respectively, would have been 21, 22, and 17 percent higher in such an eventuality."(28)

For this strategy to succeed, according to Meier, the country must possess:

1.   An abundance of natural resources and a large supply of labor. In the particular case of Peru, this condition is definitely applicable.

2.   The necessary skills to seize the opportunities brought about by comparative advantage. This implies the existence of

some degree of entrepreneurial ability and social and economic infrastructure. With respect to what types of products are likely to enjoy comparative advantages, in Peru they are refined metals and textiles; some processed agricultural goods may also have good prospects.

This strategy, however, presents serious economic constraints which greatly imperil its success. The most important, in my opinion, is that it is totally dependent on exogenous factors. These are the conditions of demand in international markets and the lowering of tariffs of the non-traditional products by the industrialized countries. The former is definitely associated with the economic cycle in the industrialized world. Being the growth rates of less-developed countries so dependent on trade with the industrialized countries, an economic recession in these countries tend to slow down considerably the growth of output in the less developed countries. In principle, as Arthur Lewis suggests, this problem has a solution if steps are undertaken to promote trade among the less developed countries(29); nevertheless, this problem is not easily solved since it involves concerted efforts to establish guidelines of trade financing and ingenuity on the part of the entrepreneurs in those countries. On the other hand, tariffs on non-traditional products have been the source of endless debates in international forums, where less developed countries have constantly exerted pressure to have the tariffs for their products lowered. Furthermore, it may be argued that the theoretical validity of the export promotion strategy could be subjected to the fallacy of composition. In other words, the fact that this strategy has benefited the countries that embraced it, (Korea, Taiwan, Singapore, etc.) does not necessarily mean that all the less developed countries that adopt it will equally benefit from it. In fact, in an empirical simulation study, William Cline shows that the generalization of this strategy "across all developing countries would result in untenable market penetration into industrial countries"(30) that would in all likelihood set off pressures in these countries to enact protective tariffs.

It is time now to incorporate some institutional factors which might hamper the success of this new mode of accumulation:

1. If the needed capital investment is primarily carried out by transnational corporations, as has occurred in Northern Mexico, Hong Kong, and Singapore, then Peru might become another "export platform", doomed to process certain parts of some products. In fact, G. Helleiner has identified these types of products as the most promising for the success of manufacturing for world markets.(31) For example, these products could be semi-conductors, valves, and components of electronic products of Japanese and American industry. Given the power of transnational corporations in the industrialized countries, Helleiner asserts, these products are unlikely to be protected by tariffs in those markets. However, for the less developed countries, this policy in essence means relinquishing control over production and marketing to these foreign concerns. If bargaining power is a factor not to be dismissed in modern economics, then this strategy

definitely leads to the weakening of the country's social institutions vis-à-vis the transnational corporate world, with the consequence of a loss in the control of economic policies.(32)

2.   Export recovery through this strategy does not always take place in the short-run. Setting aside unfavorable conditions in the world market, this strategy has been vigorously supported by Schydlowsky and Wicht who advocate the transformation of the installed industrial capacity to produce for export through the use of intensive labor shifts.(33) However, this adaptation is not that simple if one considers that the Peruvian industrial firms--protected for so long--still have to engage in technique adjustments to bring average costs down to competitive world levels for which the improvement of total productivity is necessary. Also, the strategy will demand from Peruvian entrepreneurs the mastery of marketing techniques and the search for and establishment of dependable marketing channels. This might take some time.

3.   Finally, let us consider one basic factor: the institutional behavior of the export capitalist class. In the previous section, it was stated that the expansive phase of the economic cycle was initiated by the accumulation in the export sector; of course, this implies an increase in aggregate demand which stimulates investment in the internal industrial sector. But, how can one predict the expenditure decisions originated in export income? It is most unfortunate to point out that the evidence in Peru shows that the export capitalist class and the income it generates for the upper classes is characterized by heavy expenditure on luxuries, most of them imported! This, in fact, happened in 1979 and 1980 when a sudden turnabout in world prices and the prevalence of the CERTEX led to windfall profits in the export sector. Part of these proceeds were captured by the government and were used to accelerate the repayment of the external debt. The rest, however, was mainly expended in the purchase of foreign consumer goods, whose tariffs the government lowered. In this way, the government sought to alleviate inflationary pressures by channelling consumption to cheaper foreign goods. In this sense, it was striking to see Lima invaded by luxury items while at the same time portraying the tremendous signs of the recession. Given this fact, therefore, the likelihood of developing strong linkages to the rest of the country remains very doubtful.

Finally, I would like to highlight the real nature of stabilization policies. By now, it should be obvious that the success of economic policies devised to foster the establishment of an export promotion strategy is constrained by the presence of economic and institutional constraints which are not easily resolved. What has been less obvious is the fact that the stabilization policies are not devoid of political considerations. For example, let us take the case of that variable which has wrested so much attention from us throughout this study: the exchange rate. Accordingly, the devaluation of the exchange rate is not a policy tool implemented to restore equilibrium in the external sector as conventional economic theory states. Rather, it is a <u>political</u> instrument, which in this particular case transfers income from one capitalist class (the local industrial-ists) to another class (exporters).(34) Therefore, the setting of the exchange rate responds to intra- capitalist class struggle, since its under- or overvaluation plays such a critical role in the accumulation process in both sectors; thus, an undervalued exchange rate will naturally be advocated by exporters, who see an excellent tool to keep the competitive position of their products in world markets but one which produces a contraction in aggregate demand (through a drop in the industrial real wage) that leads to a reduction in the gross domestic product. In fact, as was demonstrated in the last chapter, this was what happened in Peru. The sharp devaluation rate and related stabilization measures, such as the reduction in subsidies in real terms, led to a pronounced slump and to a redistribution of income in favor of both capitalist classes. The substantial drop in the real wage, however, acted as a stimulus for the expansion of activities in the export sector, since, as is well known, low wages make their products more competitive.

104

NOTES

(1)Jürgen Schuldt, Política Económica y Conflicto Social (Lima, Perú: Universidad del Pacífico, Centro de Investigación, 1980), p. 15.

(2)Samir Amin, Accumulation on a World Scale. A critique of the Theory of Underdevelopment, cited by Schuldt, op.cit., p.16.

(3)Thorp and Whitehead, op.cit., p. 12.

(4)Ernesto Laclau, Politics and Ideology in Marxist Theory (United Kingdom: Verso Edition, 1979), p.34.

(5)Karl Marx, Capital, A Critique of Political Economy. 3 Vols. Edited by Friedrich Engels (New York: International Publishers, 1967) Vol. I p. 35.

(6)Paul Mattick, Marx and Keynes; The Limits of the Mixed Economy (Boston: P. Sargent, 1969), p. 67.

(7)Marx, op.cit., Vol. III p.242.

(8)John Weeks, "Crisis and Accumulation in the Peruvian Economy", Review of Radical Political Economics, Vol. 8 No.4 (1976), 56-72.

(9)Pinzás García, op.cit., p. 133.

(10)Ibid., 135

(11)Joan Robinson, Economic Philosophy (Chicago: Aldine Publishing Company, 1962), p.26.

(12)R. Meek, Economics and Ideology and Other Essays; Studies in the Development of Economic Thought (London: Chapman and Hall, 1967).

(13)B. Fine, Economic Theory and Ideology (New York: Holmes and Meier Publishers, 1981).

(14)Laclau, op.cit., pp. 22-34.

(15) Alain de Janvry, "The Political Economy of Rural Development", American Journal of Agricultural Economics, Vol.57 No.3 (August 1975), 490-499.

(16)F.H. Cardozo, "The Originality of the Copy: ECLA and the Idea of Development" in Rothko Chapel, Toward a New Strategy for Development (Pergamon Press, 1979), p.55.

[17] De Janvry, op. cit., 491.

[18] Ibid., 495.

[19] Bruno Seminario and María Cruz Saco, La Naturaleza del Ciclo Económico en el Perú (Lima, Perú: Universidad del Pacífico, Centro de Investigación, 1980).

[20] Ibid., 144.

[21] Ibid., 171.

[22] Ibid., 165.

[23] A. Quijano, Nationalism and Capitalism in Peru: A Study in New Imperialism (New York and London: Monthly Review Press, 1971).

[24] Weeks, op.cit., 57-58.

[25] Bhagwati and Krueger, op.cit., 420-421.

[26] G. M. Meier, Leading Issues in Economic Development. 3rd. ed. (New York: Orxford University Press, 1976), p. 672.

[27] Bela Balassa, "Exports and Economic Growth", Journal of Development Economics, 5 (1978), 181-189.

[28] Ibid., 187.

[29] Arthur Lewis, "The Slowing Down of the Engine of Growth", The American Economic Review Vol. 70 No.4 (September 1980), 555-564.

[30] William R. Cline, "Can the East Asian Model of Development be Generalized?", World Development Vol. 10 No.2 (1982), 88.

[31] G. Helleiner, "Manufacturing Exports from Less Developed Countries and Multinational Firms", Economic Journal (March 1973), 31.

[32] This point is addressed by R. Newfarmer, "Multinationals and Marketplace Magic in the 1980s", Overseas Development Council, University of Notre Dame, (unpublished manuscript, February 1982).

[33] Schydlowsky and Wicht, op.cit.

[34] Jürgen Schuldt, "Cuánto Cuesta el Dólar?", cited by Seminario and Cruz Saco, op.cit., p. 142.

VI
Conclusions

This study has been directed towards evaluating the economic effects of devaluation on the Peruvian economy during the stabilization period of 1975-1978.

The thrust of this study was empirical. It set out to investigate specifically how the application of devaluation policies implemented during this period affected the growth of national output and the distribution of income between property owners and non-property owners. The study has conclusively demonstrated that the application of devaluation significantly reduced the growth of national output and altered the existing distribution of income in favor of the property owners. It was also demonstrated that these negative results were mostly felt during the period 1977-1978 in which free market forces were left to determine the price of foreign exchange.

The empirical results obtained were made possible through the application of Lance Taylor's model to the Peruvian economy. This model has been specifically designed to show the likely effects of devaluation on domestic product and income distribution when applied to a semi-industrialized economy. Taylor's model was selected because it does incorporate institutional features that have been largely ignored by conventional macro theory but which are definitely found in a less developed country like Peru. The most important features which are built into the model and which were found applicable to the Peruvian economy were the oligopolistic structure of the industrial sector that is characterized by mark-up pricing and the non-competitive nature of intermediate imports, in other words, imported goods which are not likely to have a locally produced substitute. Furthermore, to the extent that the consideration of income distribution is of paramount importance for the analysis of a less developed economy, Taylor's model is definitely useful since it explicitly deals with the distributional effects of income by evaluating the impact of devaluation on the functional shares of wage and profit incomes.

However, heavy reliance on Taylor's model posed limitations to the scope of this study as well. In my opinion, these limitations are mainly three:

1. The model deals with short-term phenomena, in other words it aims to measure the negative impact on the growth of

domestic output from the application of devaluation in the short-run. Therefore, it ignores long-run reallocation of resources in the direction of production of exportables that may speed up recovery.

2. The model analyzes the impact of devaluation on the growth of domestic output, ceteris paribus. That is to say, it assumes away the presence or influence of other stabilization measures that could have affected negatively the growth of output.

3. Finally, to deal with income distribution phenomena, the model uses a level of aggregation that oversimplifies the reality of Peruvian society since the informal sector is not explicitly dealt with. In order to cope with this difficulty, this study incorporated income generated in this sector within the incomes of non-property owners. It should be noted, however, that a more rigorous analysis of income distribution requires the disagreggation of this sector.

Without ignoring the importance of these limitations, it should be pointed out, however, that there exists one very important reason that merits the selection of Taylor's model. As stated in the introduction, the purpose and importance of this study lies in contrasting the approaches of both monetarists and structuralists to economic development. Taylor's model is associated with the structuralist approach, which in my opinion, provides a more accurate description of the Peruvian economy than its monetarist counterpart. This point can be supported by the fact that structuralist analysis has provided a more accurate diagnosis of the roots of the economic crisis. In order to explain this, let us first review the critical elements that originated the crisis and the set of circumstances which gave way to the application of the stabilization measures in general and devaluation in particular.

As has been stated throughout this study, the military regime intensified the policies aimed at industrialization via import substitution which has been conventionally regarded as infla-tionary. At the same time, the regime managed to undertake structural reforms which redistributed property, away from private individuals, and in favor of the state and urban and rural workers of the modern sector.

Given the presence of a healthy degree of economic wisdom on the part of state managers, the goals of the military regime and the kind of reforms it undertook seem to be appropriate for Peru. But, unfortunately, such wisdom was not present nor did the reforms contemplate the complexity of all those factors influencing the state of underdevelopment. For example, the exchange rate was overvalued for too long, urban consumers were greatly favored by price controls of vital goods (food, public transportation, etc.) and the interest rate was negative in real terms; given these facts, exporters, food producers, and private savers were most likely discouraged. On the other hand, it should have been evident to the military rulers that expropriating property of essential productive assets is not a sufficient condition for erradicating an unjust social order that prevents economic development; what is also necessary is the presence of management skills needed to run efficiently the enterprises, so that income can be generated from their operations instead of deficits.

Is it possible to assert unequivocally that the strategy of industrialization via import substitution should be held solely responsible for the magnitude of the economic disequilibrium, which by 1975 called for the application of the stabilization measures? The answer, in my opinion, is no. In Peru, it is imperative to recognize at once that inflation was never a serious problem until 1976 and, on the contrary, as has been clearly demonstrated in this study, is a new phenomenon in the economic history of the country that has been generated precisely by devaluation. To find answers that explain the magnitude of the external disequilibrium, therefore, should lead us directly to the way in which the state financed its public investment and expenditures which was done, as is well-known, by external borrowing. The importance of this point should not be ignored, for in Peru, the urgency for investment in social infrastructure is for all to see; by undertaking costly projects such as irrigation, the oil pipeline, etc., it is clear that the military realized the urgency of this need. Unfortunately, as happens in many less developed countries, public investment is often accompanied by a larger bureaucracy, waste, and corruption--features which were not absent in Peru. In the end, the goals of the government proved to be very ambitious and some of the projects ill-conceived.

Therefore, the roots of the external disequilibrium should be also placed on the massive external borrowing which started in late 1973 and which, given the long gestation periods of major public investment projects and the unrewarded expectations of oil deposits, led to a crisis of the balance of payments which was structural in nature. It is in this sense that the "visible" manifestation of the crisis of 1975 should be more properly viewed: on one hand, the large investment projects financed from abroad; on the other hand, the development strategy of the regime which was devised to foster industrialization and thus favored local industrialists and urban consumers. Given the existence of an overvalued exchange rate, generous credit terms, and high rates of protection on their products, local industrialists responded by increasing the imports of intermediate goods and machinery not intensive in the use of labor, while at the same time, seeing their oligopolistic position hardly threatened, there was little incentive to expand operations and lower the average production costs down to world competitive levels. The consequence of all this, therefore, was the presence of a strategy unlikely to solve the unemployment problem, unlikely to expand the internal market, and unlikely to generate foreign exchange.

Given the convergence of these phenomena, therefore, the crisis in the balance of payments was inevitable. The stabilization measures that were applied thereafter were in part the result of a bargaining process that set the foreign commercial banks and later the IMF, on one side, and the Peruvian Government on the other. At issue was the repayment of the external debt, whose interest charges and payments on principal had the external accounts under severe financial strain. As has been explained before, the disagreements centered around the degree or intensity of the corrective measures which ended up imposing a high social cost. It should be stressed that the Peruvian Government, by deciding to finance its ambitious projects through external borrowing, was in fact tied to the conditions set by this type of financing, in other words, it had accepted the given rules of the game. It is in this sense that the Peruvian experience could be taken as a lesson for any less developed country which chooses the capitalist money and capital markets to finance development projects. At times, as it happened in late 1973, there could be an excess supply of financial funds which definitely benefits the less developed countries since there would be a higher diversification of sources of capital. But, if the debt is incurred in the form of short-term loans, if the development projects require long gestation periods, if these projects are not tied to the export sector, if economic conditions in industrialized countries reduce the demand for exportables from less developed countries and finally, if the import bill of vital inputs is more expensive, then external disequilibrium is likely to arise. Under these circumstances, the government soon finds itself in desperate need of foreign exchange to keep importing vital inputs and to meet the payments of interests on the external debt. Often, the badly needed foreign exchange is secured after the country has agreed with the banks or with the IMF on the introduction of stabilization measures which could be very costly in economic, social, and political terms.

It is beyond any doubt, that the application of the stabilization measures brought on a negative impact on the economic welfare of the vast majority of the Peruvian population. In chapter four, it was empirically shown how the application of one particular measure (devaluation) was largely responsible for the contraction of output, for the drop of the real wage, and for the fueling of inflation. On the other hand, devaluation also generated windfall profits for exporters. In order to find answers that might explain the simultaneous occurrence of these uneven socioeconomic effects, one has to grasp the fundamentals of the very complex nature that the Peruvian economy presents.

To meet this goal, I introduced in chapter five an alternative approach, based on the concept of mode of accumulation, that incorporated institutional and political phenomena as an effort to obtain a richer understanding of the Peruvian crisis. This approach places strong emphasis on the use of Marxian models to explain economic reality. It is within this context that it is possible to reach conclusions about the applicability and legitimacy of the stabilization measures in general and devaluation in particular. To this point I turn below.

According to this alternative approach, devaluation and related stabilization measures were applied with the aim of creating the preconditions necessary to establish a new mode of accumulation, one based on export promotion. By late 1978, recovery was imminent and this trend was more visible in 1979 and

1980, when the external deficits were reversed. Impressive as the recovery in the external sector was, one has to pause and think about the costs that the stabilization measures inflicted on the underprivileged Peruvian social groups. For once, as was shown in chapter four, devaluation did play a substantial role in generating abnormally steep inflation rates that have already produced high inflationary expectations, which, however, will not negatively affect the profitability of the export sector if the exchange rate is continuously devalued. Other economic costs are already well known: less output and the deterioration of the distribution of income. Related economic costs should include the fact that the government, having decided to restore profits in general and export profitability in particular, enacted laws directed at weakening the bargaining power of the unions and thus depressing wage costs. For example, the reorganization of the "Comunidad Industrial" was quickly passed in 1976.(1) However, equally or more important is the consideration of the social costs; for devaluation has meant the sudden impoverishment of masses of Peruvians, especially those located in the peripheral urban areas. It is not difficult to visualize a situation in which workers and people with fixed incomes saw in front of them the sharp hike in the general price level that must have reduced considerably their capacity to provide even their necessaries of life. This fact, in concert with the waves of unemployed and underemployed, is surely responsible to some extent for the increased social unrest in Lima, where crime and corruption have become generalized.

At this point, it is pertinent to address the following question: was this cost necessary? In other words, were all these recessionary measures really necessary to foster recovery through the establishment of a new mode of accumulation (export promotion)? Was the introduction of these measures, that were aimed at stimulating expansion of what was thought to be the leading export sector (non-traditional products), socially and economically justifiable?

At first glance, there are strong reasons to believe that, unfortunately, the degree of these measures was unjustifiable given the influence that exogenous variables exerted upon the recovery of the external sector. It is true that exports of non-traditional products did expand considerably, but of greater influence was the recovery of traditional products, both in prices and in volume. And this, as was concluded in chapter four, took place independently of the level of aggregate demand, the level of domestic costs, and the price of the exchange rate. If this assertion is reasonable, one can conclude that, as suggested in chapter four, exporters of non-traditional products enjoyed extraordinary windfall profits, which in great part was due to the transference of income away from the workers and small businesspersons.

It is possible to think of alternative policies aimed at achieving different goals. One can think, for example, of the fact that the Peruvian authorities could have visualized a rapid improvement in the external sector derived from an enlarged export supply and from better world prices (although this is very difficult to predict); in this sense, with such recovery largely dependent on exogenous factors, a large devaluation would not have been necessary. Also, it is possible to think of a situation in which the government is committed to protecting the welfare of the Peruvian workers; in this sense, what is expected is government actions that prevent the deterioration of income distribution against workers and the control of inflation through mechanisms other than the exclusive control of wages.

In order to illustrate this, I have proceeded to carry out three empirical simulations which precisely take such alternative policies into account. Such simulations cover the period 1977-1978 since this was the period in which the impact of the stabilization policies was most greatly felt. These empirical simulations basically follow the same methodological procedures of the ones that were carried out in chapter four. In other words, the objective is to predict the level of home goods output (X_H) and gross domestic product at constant prices by simulating the actual variation in the exchange rate (e), the wage rate (w) and the terms of trade (P_x*). The simulation also provides information about the income shares and on the variations of the price level and real wage.

In the first simulation an effective devaluation rate of 50 percent is assumed rather than the one of 140 percent which was applied. The value of all the other variables remains the same. Therefore: e = 1.50

The results are shown in Table 24.

TABLE 24

ALTERNATIVE STABILIZATION POLICIES. SIMULATION No. 1

	Prediction of Chapter IV	Prediction of Alternative Policy
Home goods output (X_H)	1,148,436	1,289,291
GDP at constant prices	1,121,021	1,236,621
Income shares (labor/capital)	54/46	61/39
Price level variation	64%	40%
Wage rate variation	(-)17.41%	(-)3%

As can be seen, all major indicators show a remarkable improvement over the results obtained in the chapter four. When compared with the actual results, both home goods output and the gross domestic product at constant prices would have shown a growth rate of 8 percent.

The second simulation assumes an effective devaluation rate of 50 percent and also the introduction of taxes on profit income. It is possible to represent this by the taxation on mark-ups (Z), say at a rate of 15 percent. In chapter four, the value of Z was held constant at 0.4081. The assumed values of Z and e are therefore:

e = 1.50
Z = 0.3481
The results are shown in Table 25.

TABLE 25

ALTERNATIVE STABILIZATION POLICIES. SIMULATION NO. 2

	Prediction of Chapter IV	Prediction of Alternative Policy
X_H	1,148,436	1,309,402
GDP	1,121,021	1,253,126
Income shares (labor/capital)	54/46	64/36
Price level	64%	34%
Real wage	(−)17.41%	(+).05%

The results show an even greater improvement. The inflation rate is reduced from 40 percent to 34 percent; it is significant that this reduction is of the same rate that taxed the mark ups. There is even an improvement in the real wage rate and the income shares show variation in favor of labor. Also, when compared with the actual results of chapter four, home-goods output and the gross domestic product show a growth rate of 10 percent and 9 percent respectively.

Finally, the third simulation assumes the same effective devaluation rate (50 percent), the same tax on mark ups (15 percent) but some government transfers in favor of labor which raises nominal wages from 36 to 45 percent. Thus:

e = 1.50
Z = 0.3481
W = 1.45
The results are as follows:

TABLE 26

ALTERNATIVE STABILIZATION POLICIES. SIMULATION No. 3

	Prediction of Chapter IV	Prediction of Alternative Policy
X_H	1,148,436	1,328,110
GDP	1,121,021	1,268,480
Income shares	54/46	66/34
Price level	64%	40%
Real wage	(−)17.41%	(+)3%

    The improvement is even more evident, although the inflation
rate climbed back to 40 percent. Both the home-goods output and
GDP would have increased by 11 percent with respect to the actual
results and the distribution of income would have been even more
favorable for wage earners.
    All these points lead to the following conclusions. On one
hand, as stated in chapter four, devaluation played a largely
unnecessary role in the correction of the external disequilibrium
because the recovery of the export sector which was already
visible in 1978 was due in great part to exogenous factors such
as higher world prices of the traditional products and an enlarged
supply of these products that originated in costly investment
projects dating several years back.
    However, of much more significance is the conclusion that the
stabilization measures in general and devaluation in particular
were ill-conceived policies in the following sense: not only was
devaluation ineffective in reversing the external disequilibrium
but it also was directly responsible for an unnecesary decline in
the growth of output. In fact, as the alternative empirical
simulations have shown, a modest effective devaluation rate, in
combination with measures aimed at increasing aggregate demand
via a larger income share for the workers and, with the help of
the exogenous recovery of the export sector, would have produced
an increase in the growth of output.
    An evaluation of the theoretical rationale of a policy which
has contracted output so significantly and which has altered the
existing income distribution against non-property owners, should
therefore be undertaken in the context of the type of economic
society it aims to shape (along with related stabilization
measures) and in the context of the goals it pursues. In chapter
five, it was suggested that the stabilization measures aim at
promoting a new pattern of development, one based on the export
of non-traditional products; in the same chapter is was pointed
out that the success of this strategy is severely constrained by
economic factors and by the nature of Peruvian social institutions. On the other hand, it is within this context that the
objectives pursued by devaluation policies should be more
properly assessed: given a strategy of development that promotes
exports of non-traditional products, it was concluded that
devaluation is a political instrument aimed at transferring
economic surplus away from local industrialists to the capitalists in the export sector. In other words, it is by restoring
the profitability in the export sector that the capitalist mode
of production sees the way out from an economic crisis that is
determined by the inability of local industry to increase the
economic surplus, but whose "visible" manifestation is an external
disequilibrium. Therefore, the transference of economic resources
to the export sector is a condition for its recovery, and it
should generate an expansive phase of the economic cycle and thus
restore the dynamism of capital accumulation.
    My final thoughts are directed at discussing the role of
economic theory. Devaluation and related stabilization measures
represent in essence a return to resource allocation through the

free market mechanism. It is in this sense that they are policies identified with the principles of classical liberalism that monetarism embraces. In specific terms, the issue I want to address is the following: what is the use and applicability of conventional economic theory, --specifically of that doctrine which seems so greatly to inspire the logic of stabilization policies (monetarism)--for the reality of the Peruvian experience?

First of all, I shall state anew what has already been treated in the third chapter and what should be very obvious by now: that is, the unrelenting faith that monetarism has in the ability of free market forces to restore "equilibrium" in the economy, i.e. the convergence of aggregate supply and aggregate demand at levels of full employment of resources. An external disequilibrium, therefore, is a temporary deviation that should be quickly eliminated if free market forces are left to correct an overvalued exchange rate and at the same time depress an excessive aggregate demand that is pressing for more imports.

That was the diagnosis of the Peruvian crisis. The stabilization measures applied were meant to move the economy towards "equilibrium". As has been seen, the disequilibrium in the external sector was greatly eliminated although it is impossible to discard the great influence of exogenous factors in the recovery of the external sector. Moreover, as has been demonstrated in this study, the path to equilibrium in the external sector carried with it a shift in relative prices that implied, as Marcelo Diamand states, "greater incentives for the traditional exporting sector to the detriment of wage earners".(2) It is unlikely that such income redistribution has been regarded as socially acceptable by all Peruvians; the existence of increasing social unrest on the part of wage earners is evidence of this point.

It is very important to bear in mind that, underneath the strict definition of the key variables for which monetarism characterizes a market economy, lies a specific vision of the world which reflects, in my opinion, two fundamental themes:

1. The first point is related to what was briefly stated in the third chapter: the problem of theory ladenness, in other words, the conscious or unconscious manipulation of the subject matter to mirror the theory, thus, the loss of objectivity. For example, inflation is seen as a demand pull phenomenon; in this study, however, it was seen that inflation would be more properly attributed to cost push factors. However, this issue takes on much more relevance by exploring how monetarism defines economic concepts and sets the limits of analysis. To illustrate, it should be remembered that Seminario and Cruz Saco point out the recurrent crisis in the balance of payments as a serious obstacle to the process of accumulation. In structuralist terms, this fact could be described as the presence of external bottlenecks, in other words, economic factors that "lower the dynamic efficiency of the whole system".(3) However, as Diamand clearly points out, traditional theory (monetarism) ignores this fact because full employment of resources is "defined at the level of utilization of the scarcest item" (foreign exchange).(4) Therefore, he goes on,

"bottlenecks do not exist [since] any production that exceeds [this] redefined level of full employment becomes overexpansion."(5) In this sense, therefore, "unemployment of resources does not exist [and the expected] income redistribution is not recessive, [rather] it is the return to the distribution compatible with real possibilities".(6)

2. The second point I would like to address is associated with the first one. Conventional economic theory in general and monetarism in particular are bodies of thought which have been devised to respond to economic realities of advanced market societies. It is very important, therefore, to evaluate the applicability of the theory to the economic reality of a less developed country like Peru, with characteristics so far different from the ones in an advanced market society.

In general terms, the evaluation of the applicability of any theory demands the consideration of two factors: (a) first, one has to consider the validity of the premises, which depict, as an initial approximation, the basic assumptions and characteristics that prevail in the economy under investigation; and (b) based on such premises, how accurately does the theory describe the actual functioning of the economy.

In the case of a positivist methodology, on which the monetarist theory is based, the first factor does not have as much importance as the second. Despite the disregard for assumptions, however, implicit in the monetarist view is the presence of rationality in any market economy, which if left unhampered by government authorities, will efficiently guide individuals in their decisions to optimally assign their economic resources. From this vision of society, therefore, it is possible to postulate laws about economic behavior and thus predict it. Given this basic criteria, the goal of the theory becomes just to describe as accurately as possible the complex reality of an economic system, however narrowly defined; in this sense, the theory is an instrument used for explanation.

On the other hand, this picture becomes more complex when it is realized that economic theories develop a set of policy prescriptions which are implemented upon recommendation. Since this implies the active participation of the economist in the social arena, there must exist some sort of moral, ethical, or "scientific" justification that would serve to legitimize the recommended policies, especially if the latter affect the welfare of some groups of individuals in society. The way a positivist stance solves this dilemma is by postulating that "goodness" resides in how well one can describe what actually happens (in the case of the economic scientist) and, in the case of the economist as a politician this "goodness" will be related to denouncing (advocating) all those policies that hamper (enhance) the economic conditions that characterize a natural order. In the specific case of monetarism, for example, the natural order is nothing but the freedom of the individuals, which is determined by their unfettered maximizing economic decisions that can only take place within a market economy.

With all these points in mind, I shall now proceed to
evaluate this methodological approach with respect to Peruvian
reality. I shall start by citing two concrete examples.

First, let us consider the most visible expression of the
crisis, that is, the disequilibrium in the external sector. In
plain language, the period 1975-1978 can be depicted as one in
which the country, for all practical purposes lacked foreign
exchange, since reserves had rapidly dwindled. As one former
minister put it, "there were no dollars".(7) In these circumstances, the diagnosis of the theory was very simple: the demand
for foreign exchange had greatly outstripped the supply of it,
and this scarcity had become critical. Therefore, a set of
policies were prescribed in order to stimulate the supply of
foreign exchange.

In pure economic analysis, of course, this makes sense and
such a set of policies should be viewed as appropriate. But,
nevertheless, it is seldom investigated who are the actual
participants in the market for foreign exchange and what specific
economic actions or decisions these participants undertake through
the use of this scarce item, which, as is well known, plays a
significant role in any development effort. For example, it was
stated in chapter five that the suppliers of foreign exchange
(exporters) spend their proceeds on luxuries. With regard to
those who demand foreign exchange i.e., local industrialists, it
is equally important to evaluate the specific use of it, for
example, will they consume it or invest it? Will they buy labor-
saving machinery? Finally, despite the importance that foreign
exchange has for the whole country, it has been actually demonstrated that small groups have a relatively large control over
the use of foreign exchange, thus exerting power over the rest of
society. For example, the top 10 percent of the families in
national income use 39 percent of total foreign exchange, and the
top 20 percent use 53 percent of it.(8)

The other example I would like to mention is the following:
as is well-known, a too vigorous industrialization via import
substitution has been characterized as shifting resources away
from rural areas to the benefit of the urban areas because the
internal terms of trade are adverse to dwellers in the countryside. In Peru, this fact has become very evident, as is illustrated by the massive migration to cities and by the increasing imports of food. Devaluation could partially reverse this
trend by encouraging the production of food for export in the
countryside. However, how is it possible to conclude that Peruvian farmers will react positively and rapidly when the countryside is so desperately in need of an adequate social infrastructure?

The goal of citing these two examples has been to gradually
introduce the kind of setting in which the market institution has
to operate in Peru. To make this point explicit, one should
remember that Peru is plagued by the interaction of a modern and
a traditional sector; in the former, market social relations
prevail, whereas in the latter such relations are not that
obvious. Now, and this is a very important point to bear in mind,

for monetarism this complex phenomena is reduced by postulating
the existence of one market. In other words, all analysis is
mainly devoted to the study of the real economic possibilities
existing in the money economy (the capitalist sector) and thus,
implicitly assumes away the set of institutions that exist in the
little developed money economy (the pre-capitalist sector).
Considering this, a very serious problem arises, unfortunately,
when one looks in some detail into the specific socioeconomic
shape that Peruvian reality presents. For example, in the
capitalist sector, one cannot ignore the oligopolistic market
structure that the local industry has; in this sense any policies
aimed at promoting efficiency through free market forces could
well end up strengthening the power of the oligopolies at the
expense of other sectors of the population.

    This argument is equally important when the economic and
political consequences of the stabilization policies are brought
into consideration. If the latter lead to the establishment and
predominance of a new mode of accumulation (export promotion)
--as definitely happened in Chile and Argentina--then not only is
it necessary to exert political will to carry it out, but it is
also crucial to have a theory useful to legitimize the policies
before society. Jürgen Schuldt associates monetarism with this
new economic trend that has been increasingly making inroads in
Peru.(9) In my opinion, such association is overstated if the
economic success of export promotion crucially depends on a
persistent undervalued exchange rate; monetarism, as is well
known, preaches the free interaction of market forces to set
prices. Nevertheless, there are specific policies advocated by
exporters which find theoretical support and legitimation in such
doctrine; for example, one can cite the need for a balanced
budget to head off inflationary pressures; the establishment of
free trade policies and the rule of the principle of comparative
advantage. In the case of Peru, the latter implies the use of
techniques of production based on the intensive utilization of
the cheapest factor, in other words, labor. Unfortunately, the
social legitimation from the use of monetarist policies for the
benefit of export promotion is definitely put in doubt if de
Janvry's theoretical framework is applicable to Peru. For, as
might well be remembered, the latter stresses the presence of
miserably low wages as a necessary condition for the success of
capital accumulation in backward countries.

    Therefore, with all these points in mind, it is possible to
discern more clearly the role of economic theory in the process
of economic development, that, in the case of Peru, is proving to
be so costly as is evidenced by the magnitude of the crisis of
1975. To select the market institution as a guide for resource
allocation (at least in some sectors of the economy) will necessarily demand the use of a theoretical framework to help authorities devise policies on sound analytical basis. In fact, for any
country that chooses an export-oriented or free trade strategy of
development there seems to be no choice other than to adjust
domestic production costs to international levels so as to have
the products remain competitive; the selective and regulated use

of the market institution could be a good tool to achieve this
goal and, in this sense, economic theory could prove to be an
invaluable instrument for efficient decision-making, both at the
national and firm levels. However, on the other hand, economic
theory could be used as an instrument to legitimize an existing
social economic order. For example, the Chile of post-1974 has
witnessed the rigid use of the theory which prevailed before
Keynes; at the moment of this writing (1982), recession in world
markets has negatively affected an economy which based all her
success on the dynamism of the export promotion strategy. The
loss in output and the increase in the unemployment rate are
tackled through deflationary policies, such as budget cuts and
even lower nominal wages. This surprising faith in the classical
doctrine in reality masks the existence of social conflict, for
workers and capitalists do not share equally the burden of the
crisis. By the same token, in Peru, the launching of an export
promotion strategy and thus, the more systematic use of monetarist
policies, could strengthen precisely those features that make an
unfettered market mechanism an institution of unequal exchange
and oppression, as de Janvry points out. In this case, monetarism
is clearly an instrument useful to legitimize and perpetuate an
unjust socioeconomic order.

This last point should serve to underscore the importance of
a tenet which has been present throughout this study. This is
the fact that stabilization policies based on monetarist theory
are, in my opinion, ill-conceived to grasp the essence of Peruvian economic reality and thus to tackle efficiently the economic
crisis. If the avowed goal of Peruvian society is to reduce
poverty, lower unemployment, and create the basis for a more
egalitarian society with rapid economic growth, then the country
has no other choice but to rationalize the state intervention in
the economic arena, something strongly opposed by monetarists.
That intervention could materialize in the form of discouraging
the consumption of luxuries, of encouraging the intensive use of
labor, of elevating the skills of workers, of taxing the windfall
profits and using the proceeds to build the social infrastructure
that poor peasants desperately need, etc. Otherwise, the free
market mechanism will remain an instrument to perpetuate the mis-
use of political, ideological, and economic power. As long as
monetarism does not recognize this fact, then it should be
discarded as a viable alternative that aims at fostering development while at the same time rooting out inequality. It is not
enough to advocate free trade and thus defend and protect the
sovereignity of the consumer. For a less developed country it is
more important to visualize how the uncontrolled import of
luxuries might drain reserves and thus imperil the financial
situation of the external sector. It is even more important to
analyze in the first place how the incomes that can purchase
those goods are generated, and what factors can explain their
occurrence. In this way, appropriate theoretical tools could be
constructed and put to the service of the goal of creating a more
just society.

NOTES

[1]The law creating the "Comunidad Industrial" was originally passed in 1970 and it sought to give workers not only participation in profits but also in equity. This set off strong protests from the local industrialists. In 1976, in order to appease this group, the government substantially reformed the law, reducing the degree of worker participation.

[2]Marcelo Diamand, "Towards a Change in the Economic Paradigm Through the Experience of Developing Countries", Journal of Development Economics 5 (1978), 36.

[3]Ibid., 32

[4]Ibid., 34

[5]Ibid.

[6]Ibid.

[7]Conversation of the author with Javier Silva Ruete, former Minister of the Treasury.

[8]Amat y León, op.cit., p. 84.

[9]Schuldt, op.cit.

Epilogue

Recent economic events dramatize the extent of the dependency of the Peruvian economy upon the industrialized world. They also prove, on the other hand, that there is little room for maneuvering in the application of economic policy and, more importantly perhaps, accentuates the lack of imagination and creativity in formulating concrete alternative policies which might lessen the burden of the external debt and stimulate economic recovery in the short-run.

The current economic plight of most Latin American countries suggests how little these countries and the international commercial banks learned from the Peruvian experience which anteceded the current events by almost seven years. Mexico, Brazil, Argentina, Chile, and Venezuela, to cite the most dramatic cases, financed economic expansion by external borrowing. Each country is presently experiencing increasing difficulties in meeting payments on their foreign debt. The situation is so delicate that it has threatened the stability of international trade and finance, not to mention the political stability of the particular Latin American regimes. The financial crises in these countries increasingly resemble that of New York City in 1975, during which the City, facing repayment of debts and dwindling revenues, implemented drastic cuts in most public services in order to service the debt. Ruling out default, this will most likely be the chosen response of Peru and the rest of the Latin American countries for some years to come.

One of the oddities of the present Latin American crises is that, ignoring for the moment external factors, they were generated internally by opposing development strategies. From 1968 to 1975 Peru, as Mexico and Brazil in recent years, implemented economic policies characterized by government planning and active intervention in the external sector, in capital formation, and in the manipulation of relative prices. Chile and Argentina, on the other hand, relied more on the private sector and liberalized most sectors of the economy (Chile to a greater extent) to allow for the free play of market forces. This suggests that the recurrent economic crises in the Latin American countries require the consideration of factors that are independent of the adopted development strategy. Blaming these factors entirely on external

variables, on the other hand, is not realistic, since capitulating to the temptation to eliminate dependency upon the industrialized world--à la Cuba--does not guarantee the unleashing of indigenous forces that could foster development as rationally as possible and at minimum economic cost.

Nevertheless, the presence of external factors is pervasive and impossible to ignore. In recent years, adverse economic events have caused a deterioration in the overall economic situation in Peru while they have concurrently sharpened the distinction between the economic goals of property and non-property owners. The most negative factor has been a decline in exports brought about by a drop in the world price of Peru's traditional exports and by protectionist tendencies in the United States, adversely affecting the exports of non-traditional products, particularly textiles. This, coupled with a recovery in the demand for imports from the depressed levels of 1976-1979, has reversed the surpluses in the balance of trade.

How has the new civilian government, installed in 1980, responded to these developments? First of all, the government has not been reluctant to use more short-term external borrowing to finance current account deficits in addition to the expansion plans and working capital needs of state enterprises. Of greater interest, however, is the evaluation of long-term development goals and economic policies or strategies that are being implemented to achieve them. With regard to the former, it may be emphatically asserted that, in the presence of an external public debt that accounts for 37 percent of the gross domestic product, a service of this debt amounting to 60 percent of exports, plus an economic recession in the industrialized world, long-term development goals have been ruled out for all practical purposes. These facts of economic reality place strong constraints on a heavily dependent economy. Government policy, therefore, is limited to the urgency of short-term considerations aimed at meeting external debt payments to ensure their ability to secure additional loans. This clarifies the nature of the second issue, namely, the economic policies being implemented. Since 1980 Peru has been gradually approaching a laissez-faire type of strategy while still retaining some interventionist policies. The move toward market policies is reflected in the steady reduction of tariffs and the elimination of import restrictions placed on capital and consumer goods. By 1981 this relaxation of restrictions boosted imports dramatically, leading to deficits in the current account. In addition, subsidies for many products marketed by state enterprises had been eliminated. In contrast, this government was committed since its inception to expanding public works programs which increased the fiscal deficit as a percentage of gross domestic product from 1.5 percent in 1979 to 6.6 percent by the end of 1982. The government is still reluctant to liberalize the interest rates, bowing to pressures from local industrialists and the construction sector.

The above points out a basic conflict about the conduct of economic policy and also the questions that remain; i.e., the type of pattern of growth and appropriation of wealth desired. This

is evident in the rate of inflation that is now approaching 90 percent annually. Strictly economic causes, such as the fiscal budget deficit, the role of expectations, the "imported" inflation and the rate of devaluation, cannot obscure the fact that there is a strong political component in the current inflation. The mini-devaluations that are continually being implemented account for approximately 35 percent of the inflation rate. In the face of a stagnant world demand for traditional exports the current devaluation rate aims to first protect the incomes and profit margins of exporters, rather than to stimulate recovery or expansion.

Thus, Peru is experiencing the application of policies with differing visions and goals. As suggested above, this reflects unresolved conflicts, aggravated by the burden of the external constraint. But it also demonstrates the lack of alternative proposals aimed at resolving the crisis in the short-run. Additional evidence of the vacuum this has created is provided by the platform of the political opposition--associated primarily with Socialists ideals--offering proposals for the material improvement of the disposessed in the long run. The debate centers on the types of development strategies and social institutions needed to shape future Peruvian society. In the short-run, however, given the structural dependency of the Peruvian economy, impotence and/or ignorance prevails both within the government and without.

Bibliography

Actualidad Económica. (monthly publication) Lima, Perú.

Amat y León, Ch. Carlos. La Economía de la Crisis Peruana. Lima, Perú: Fundación Friedrich Ebert, 1978.

Bacharach, Miguel. "Degree of Monopoly and Income Distribution in Three Branches of the Peruvian Manufacturing Sector". Unpublished Master's dissertation, 1980.

Balassa, Bela. "Exports and Economic Growth", Journal of Development Economics, 5 (1978), pp. 181-189.

Banco Central de Reserva del Perú. Aide Memoire on the Economic Stabilization Program of Peru. Lima, Perú, 1976.

-----. Cuentas Nacionales del Perú 1960-1974. Lima, Peru, 1976.

-----. Memoria (yearly publication), Lima, Perú.

Bhagwati, Jagdish N. Foreign Trade Regimes and Economic Development: Anatomy and Consequences of Exchange Control Regimes. New York: National Bureau of Economic Research, 1978

-----, and Krueger, A. "Exchange Control, Liberalization and Economic Development", American Economic Review, Papers and Proceedings (May 1973), pp. 419-427.

Boloña, Carlos. La Aplicación de un Modelo Econométrico a la Economía Peruana: Un Ejercicio Metodológico. Lima, Perú: Universidad del Pacífico, Centro de Investigación, 1976.

Brundenius, Claes. "Concentración de la Producción y Estructura de la Propiedad". Informe No. 040-76. Lima, Perú: Instituto Nacional de Planificación/INP-OIP, 1976.

Cabrera, César Humberto. "Perú: La Crisis y la Política de Estabilización". Lima, Perú: Fundación Friedrich Ebert, Serie Materiales de Trabajo No. 17. 1978.

Cline, William R. and Sidney Weintraub, editors. Economic Stabilization in Developing Countries. Washington, D.C.: The Brookings Institution, 1981

-----. "Can the East-Asian Model of Development be Generalized?", World Development, Vol.10 No.2 (1982), pp. 80-89.

124

Cooper, Richard N. "Currency Devaluations in Developing Countries" Essays in International Finance, No.86, International Finance Section, Department of Economics, Princeton University, Princeton, N.J., 1971.

Comisión Económica para América Latina (CEPAL), Perú: 1968-1977: La Política Económica en un Proceso de Cambio Global. Santiago, Chile: 1981.

Dernburg, Thomas F. and McDougall, Duncan M. Macroeconomics. 5th ed. Mc Graw-Hill, Inc., 1976.

Devlin, Robert. Los Bancos Trasnacionales y el Financiamiento Externo de América Latina: La Experiencia del Perú 1965-1976. Santiago, Chile: Comisión Económica para América Latina (CEPAL), 1980.

Diamand, Marcelo. "Towards a Change in the Economic Paradigm Through the Experience of Developing Countries", Journal of Development Economics, 5 (1978), pp. 19-53.

Díaz-Alejandro, Carlos F. "A Note on the Impact of Devaluation and the Redistributive Effect", Journal of Political Economy, 71 (1963), pp. 577-580.

-----. "Southern Cone Stabilization Plans". Yale University: Economic Growth Center, Paper No.330, 1979.

Eichner, Alfred S., and Kregel, J.A. "An Essay on Post-Keynesian Theory: A New Paradigm in Economics", Journal of Economic Literature, 8 (1975), pp. 1293-1314.

Fine, Benjamin. Economic Theory and Ideology. New York: Holmes and Meier Publishers, 1981.

Fitzgerald, E.V.K. The Political Economy of Peru 1956-1978. London Cambridge University Press, 1979.

Foxley, Alejandro. Experimentos Neoliberales en América Latina. Santiago, Chile: Colección Estudios CIEPLAN, No.59, 1982.

Galeano, Eduardo. Open Veins of Latin America; Five Centuries of the Pillage of a Continent. New York: Monthly Review Press, 1973.

González Izquierdo, Jorge. Perú: Una Economia en Crisis. Interpretación y Bases para una Solución. 4th ed. Lima, Perú: Universidad del Pacífico, Centro de Investigación, 1980.

Helleiner, G. "Manufacturing Exports from Less Developed Countries and Multinational Firms", Economic Journal, (March 1973), pp. 21-47.

Instituto Nacional de Estadística. Cuentas Nacionales del Perú 1950-1980. Lima, Peru, 1981.

-----. Cuentas Nacionales del Perú 1950-1978. Lima, Perú, 1979.

-----. "Algunas Consideraciones Sobre el Sector Externo". Informe No.039-76. Lima, Perú, INP-OIP, 1976.

Janvry de, Alain. "The Political Economy of Rural Development", American Journal of Agricultural Economics, Vol.57 No.3 (August 1975), pp. 490-499.

Johnson, Harry G. "The Monetary Approach to Balance of Payments Theory", Journal of Financial and Quantitative Analysis 7 (1972), pp. 1555-1572.

-----. "Elasticity, Absorption, Keynesian Multiplier, Keynesian Policy, and Monetary Approaches to Devaluation Theory: A Simple Geometrical Exposition", American Economic Review, 66 (1976), 448-452.

Kalecki, Michael. Selected Essays in the Dynamics of the Capitalist Economy, 1930-1970, Cambridge, England: Cambridge University Press, 1971.

Kreinin, Mordechai, and Officer, Lawrence H. "The Monetary Approach to the Balance of Payments: A Survey", Princeton Studies in International Finance No. 43, 1978.

-----. International Economics: A Policy Approach. 3rd ed. New York: Harcourt Brace Jovanovic, 1979.

Lewis, Arthur. "The Slowing Down of the Engine of Growth", The American Economic Review, Vol.70 No.4 (September 1980), pp. 555-564.

Krueger, Anne O. Foreign Trade Regimes and Economic Development: Liberalization Attempts and Consequences. New York: National Bureau of Economic Research, 1978.

Laclau, Ernesto. Politics and Ideology in Marxist Theory. United Kingdom: Verso Edition, 1979.

Marx, Karl. Capital, A Critique of Political Economy. 3 Vols. Edited by Friedrich Engels. New York: International Publishers, 1967.

Mattick, Paul. Marx and Keynes; The Limits of the Mixed Economy. Boston: P. Sargent, 1969.

Meek, Ronald. Economics and Ideology and Other Essays; Studies in the Development of Economic Thought. London: Chapman and Hall, 1967.

Meier, Gerald M. Leading Issues in Economic Development. 3rd
ed. New York: Oxford University Press, 1976.

Newfarmer, R. "Multinationals and Marketplace Magic in the 1980s",
University of Notre Dame: Overseas Development Council,
(February 1982).

Organización de los Estados Americanos (OEA). Informes Económicos
de Corto Plazo, Vol. VII, 1981, Perú. Washington, D.C.,
1981.

Organización Internacional del Trabajo (OIT) Perú: Estrategia de
Desarrollo y Grado de Satisfacción de las Necesidades
Básicas, 1978

Perú Económico. (monthly publication) Lima, Perú.

Pinzás García, Teobaldo. La Economía Peruana 1950-1978: Un Ensayo
Bibliográfico. Lima, Perú: Instituto de Estudios
Peruanos, 1981.

Quijano, Aníbal. Nationalism and Capitalism in Peru: A Study in
New Imperialism. New York and London: Monthly Review
Press, 1971.

Robinson, Joan. Economic Philosophy. Chicago: Aldine Publishing
Company, 1962.

Rothko Chapel. Toward a New Strategy for Development.
Pergamon Press, 1979.

Schuldt, Jürgen. Politica Económica y Conflicto Social. Lima,
Peru: Universidad del Pacífico, Centro de Investigación,
1980.

Schydlowsky, Daniel y Juan Wicht. Anatomía de un Fracaso Económico 1968-1978, Lima, Perú: Universidad del Pacífico,
Centro de Investigación, 1979.

Seminario, Bruno and Cruz Saco, María. La Naturaleza del Ciclo
Económico en el Perú. Lima, Perú: Universidad del Pacífico, Centro de Investigación, 1980.

Sheahan, John. "Peru: International Economic Policies and
Structural Change 1968-1978." Unpublished manuscript.

Taylor, Lance, and Paul Krugman, "Contractionary Effects of
Devaluation", Journal of International Economics 8
(1978), pp. 445-456.

------. Macro Models for Developing Countries, McGraw-Hill Inc.
1979.

The World Bank. Perú: Principales Cuestiones y Recomendaciones en Materia de Desarrollo. Washington, D.C., 1981.

Thorp,   Rosemary and Geoffrey Bertram. Peru 1890-1977: Growth and Policy in an Open Economy. New York: Columbia University Press, 1978.

-----,   and L. Whitehead. Inflation and Stabilization In Latin America. New York: Holmes and Meier Publishers, 1979.

-----,   Boloña, Carlos, and Herzka, Claudio. "The Balance of Payments Adjustment Problem in Peru". Unpublished manuscript, 1978.

Vane, Howard R., and Thomson, J. L. Monetarism: Theory, Evidence and Practice. Oxford: Martin Robertson, 1980.

Weeks, John. "Crisis and Accumulation in the Peruvian Economy 1967-1975". Review of Radical Political Economics 8:(4) (1976), pp.56-72.